INS 21 Course Guide

Property and Liability Insurance Principles
5th Edition

The Institutes
720 Providence Road, Suite 100
Malvern, Pennsylvania 19355-3433

© 2008
American Institute For Chartered Property Casualty Underwriters

All rights reserved. This book or any part thereof may not be reproduced without the written permission of the copyright holder.

Unless otherwise apparent, examples used in The Institutes materials related to this course are based on hypothetical situations and are for educational purposes only. The characters, persons, products, services, and organizations described in these examples are fictional. Any similarity or resemblance to any other character, person, product, services, or organization is merely coincidental. The Institutes are not responsible for such coincidental or accidental resemblances.

This material may contain Internet Web site links external to The Institutes. The Institutes neither approve nor endorse any information, products, or services to which any external Web sites refer. Nor do The Institutes control these Web sites' content or the procedures for Web site content development.

The Institutes specifically disclaim any implied warranties of merchantability or fitness for a particular purpose. No warranty may be created or extended by sales representatives or written sales materials.

The Institutes materials related to this course are provided with the understanding that The Institutes are not engaged in rendering legal, accounting, or other professional service. Nor are The Institutes explicitly or implicitly stating that any of the processes, procedures, or policies described in the materials are the only appropriate ones to use. The advice and strategies contained herein may not be suitable for every situation.

5th Edition • 4th Printing • January 2011

ISBN 978-0-89463-375-1

Contents

Study Materials. iii
Student Resources iv
Using This Course Guide iv
INS Advisory Committee vi
Assignments
 1. Insurance: What Is It? 1.1
 2. Who Provides Insurance and How Is It Regulated?. 2.1
 3. Measuring the Financial Performance of Insurers 3.1
 4. Marketing 4.1
 5. Underwriting 5.1
 6. Claims. 6.1
 7. Insurance Contracts 7.1
 8. Property Loss Exposures and Policy Provisions 8.1
 9. Liability Loss Exposures and Policy Provisions. 9.1
10. Managing Loss Exposures: Risk Management. 10.1
Exam Information 1

Study Materials Available for INS 21

Constance M. Luthardt and Eric A. Wiening, *Property and Liability Insurance Principles*, 4th ed., 2005, AICPCU.
INS 21 *Course Guide*, 5th ed., 2008, AICPCU (includes access code for SMART Online Practice Exams).
INS 21 SMART Study Aids—Review Notes and Flash Cards, 4th ed.

Student Resources

Catalog A complete listing of our offerings can be found in *Succeed,* The Institutes' professional development catalog, including information about:

- Current programs and courses
- Current textbooks, course guides, SMART Study Aids, and online offerings
- Program completion requirements
- Exam registration

To obtain a copy of the catalog, visit our Web site at www.TheInstitutes.org or contact Customer Service at (800) 644-2101.

How to Prepare for Institutes Exams This free handbook is designed to help you by:

- Giving you ideas on how to use textbooks and course guides as effective learning tools
- Providing steps for answering exam questions effectively
- Recommending exam-day strategies

The handbook is printable from the Student Services Center on The Institutes' Web site at www.TheInstitutes.org, or available by calling Customer Service at (800) 644-2101.

Educational Counseling Services To ensure that you take courses matching both your needs and your skills, you can obtain free counseling from The Institutes by:

- E-mailing your questions to advising@TheInstitutes.org
- Calling an Institutes' counselor directly at (610) 644-2100, ext. 7601
- Obtaining and completing a self-inventory form, available on our Web site at www.TheInstitutes.org or by contacting Customer Service at (800) 644-2101

Exam Registration Information As you proceed with your studies, be sure to arrange for your exam.

- Visit our Web site at www.TheInstitutes.org/forms to access and print the Registration Booklet, which contains information and forms needed to register for your exam.
- Plan to register with The Institutes well in advance of your exam.

How to Contact The Institutes For more information on any of these publications and services:

- Visit our Web site at www.TheInstitutes.org
- Call us at (800) 644-2101 or (610) 644-2100 outside the U.S.
- E-mail us at customerservice@TheInstitutes.org
- Fax us at (610) 640-9576
- Write to us at The Institutes, Customer Service, 720 Providence Road, Suite 100, Malvern, PA 19355-3433

Using This Course Guide

This course guide will help you learn the course content and prepare for the exam.

Each assignment in this course guide typically includes the following components:

Educational Objectives These are the most important study tools in the course guide. Because all of the questions on the exam are based on the Educational Objectives, the best way to study for the exam is to focus on these objectives.

Each Educational Objective typically begins with one of the following action words, which indicate the level of understanding required for the exam:

Analyze—Determine the nature and the relationship of the parts.

Apply—Put to use for a practical purpose.

Associate—Bring together into relationship.

Calculate—Determine numeric values by mathematical process.

Classify—Arrange or organize according to class or category.

Compare—Show similarities and differences.

Contrast—Show only differences.

Define—Give a clear, concise meaning.

Describe—Represent or give an account.

Determine—Settle or decide.

Evaluate—Determine the value or merit.

Explain—Relate the importance or application.

Identify or list—Name or make a list.

Illustrate—Give an example.

Justify—Show to be right or reasonable.

Paraphrase—Restate in your own words.

Recommend—Suggest or endorse something to be used.

Summarize—Concisely state the main points.

Outline The outline lists the topics in the assignment. Read the outline before the required reading to become familiar with the assignment content and the relationships of topics.

Key Words and Phrases These words and phrases are fundamental to understanding the assignment and have a common meaning for those working in insurance. After completing the required reading, test your understanding of the assignment's Key Words and Phrases by writing their definitions.

Review Questions The review questions test your understanding of what you have read. Review the Educational Objectives and required reading, then answer the questions to the best of your ability. When you are finished, check the answers at the end of the assignment to evaluate your comprehension.

Application Questions These questions continue to test your knowledge of the required reading by applying what you've studied to "hypothetical" real-life situations. Again, check the suggested answers at the end of the assignment to review your progress.

Sample Exam Your course guide includes a sample exam (located at the back) or a code for accessing SMART Online Practice Exams (which appears on the inside back cover). Use the option available for the course you're taking to become familiar with the test format.

For courses that offer SMART Online Practice Exams, you can either download and print a sample credentialing exam or take full practice exams using questions like those that will appear on your credentialing exam. SMART Online Practice Exams are as close as you can get to experiencing an actual exam before taking one.

More Study Aids

The Institutes also produce supplemental study tools, called SMART Study Aids, for many of our courses. When SMART Study Aids are available for a course, they are listed on page iii of the course guide. SMART Study Aids include Review Notes and Flash Cards and are excellent tools to help you learn and retain the information in each assignment.

INS Advisory Committee

Patricia M. Arnold, CPCU, ALCM
McCombs School of Business University of Texas at Austin

Gary Grasmann
Insurance Services Office, Inc.

Christine A. Sullivan, CPCU, AIM
Allstate Insurance Company

Jeffrey A. Svestka, CPCU, ARe
Fireman's Fund Insurance Co.

Marcia Tepp, CPCU, ARM, ARP, AIAF, CPIW
Sentry Insurance

Andrew Zagrzejewski, CPCU, CLU, AIC
Farmers Insurance

Assignment 1   Insurance: What Is It?

Assignment 2   Who Provides Insurance and How Is It Regulated?

Assignment 3   Measuring the Financial Performance of Insurers

Segment A is the first of three segments in the INS 21 course. These segments are designed to help structure your study.

Direct Your Learning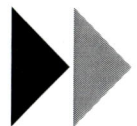

ASSIGNMENT 1

Insurance: What Is It?

Educational Objectives

After learning the content of this assignment, you should be able to:

1. Describe the role of insurance in risk management.
   A way to fin
2. Explain how insurance works as a transfer system.
3. Explain how the law of large numbers operates and applies to insurance.
4. Describe the major types of loss exposures.
5. Describe the characteristics of an ideally insurable loss exposure.
6. Explain why government insurance is needed, and give examples of federal insurance programs and state insurance programs.
7. Describe the major business operations of insurers.
8. Explain why and how state insurance departments regulate insurers.
9. Describe the benefits of insurance.
10. Describe the costs of insurance.
11. Distinguish among the major types of property and liability insurance.
12. Distinguish among the major types of life and health insurance.
13. Define or describe each of the Key Words and Phrases for this assignment.

Study Materials

Required Reading:
- Property and Liability Insurance Principles
  - Chapter 1

Study Aids:
- SMART Online Practice Exams
- SMART Study Aids
  - Review Notes and Flash Cards—Assignment 1

1.1

Outline

- **Insurance as a Risk Management Technique**
- **Insurance as a Transfer System**
  - A. Transferring the Costs of Losses
  - B. Sharing the Costs of Losses
  - C. Types of Loss Exposures
    1. Property Loss Exposures
    2. Liability Loss Exposures
    3. Personal and Personnel Loss Exposures
  - D. Ideally Insurable Loss Exposures
    1. Loss Exposure Involves Pure, Not Speculative, Risk
    2. Loss Exposure Is Subject to Accidental Loss From the Insured's Standpoint
    3. Loss Exposure Is Subject to Losses That Are Definite in Time and That Are Measurable
    4. Loss Exposure Is One of a Large Number of Similar, But Independent, Exposures
    5. Loss Exposure Is Not Subject to a Loss That Would Simultaneously Affect Many Other Similar Loss Exposures; Loss Would Not Be Catastrophic
    6. Loss Exposure Is Economically Feasible to Insure
- **Insurance as a Business**
  - A. Types of Insurers
    1. Private Insurers
    2. Federal Government Insurance Programs
    3. State Government Insurance Programs
  - B. Insurer Operations
  - C. Financial Performance of Insurers
  - D. State Insurance Regulation
  - E. Benefits of Insurance
    1. Indemnifying for Losses
    2. Reducing Uncertainty
    3. Promoting Loss Control
    4. Using Resources Efficiently
    5. Providing Support for Credit
    6. Satisfying Legal Requirements
    7. Satisfying Business Requirements
    8. Providing a Source of Investment Funds
    9. Reducing Social Burdens
  - F. Costs of Insurance
    1. Premiums Paid by Insureds
    2. Operating Costs of Insurers
    3. Opportunity Costs
    4. Increased Losses
    5. Increased Lawsuits
- **Insurance as a Contract**
  - A. Property Insurance
  - B. Liability Insurance
  - C. Life Insurance
  - D. Health Insurance
- **Summary**

Don't spend time on material you have already mastered. The SMART Review Notes are organized by the Educational Objectives found in each assignment to help you track your study.

Insurance: What Is It? 1.3

For each assignment, you should define or describe each of the Key Words and Phrases and answer each of the Review and Application Questions.

> # Educational Objective 1
> Describe the role of insurance in risk management.

Key Word or Phrase

Loss exposure (p. 1.3)

Review Question

1-1. What are some typical options used by persons or organizations to manage risk? (p. 1.4)

> # Educational Objective 2
> Explain how insurance works as a transfer system.

Review Questions

2-1. Explain why insurance is described as a transfer system. (pp. 1.4–1.5)

2-2. How do insurance buyers transfer the costs of their losses to insurance companies? (pp. 1.4–1.5)

2-3. How does insurance spread the cost of losses among all insureds? (p. 1.5)

Application Question

2-4. Assume that a new colony was established on an island as yet unclaimed by any country. The colonists each agree to help one another rebuild their homes in the event that one of the homes is damaged or destroyed. In what way does this agreement compare to a system of insurance? (pp. 1.4–1.5)

Insurance: What Is It?   1.5

Educational Objective 3
Explain how the law of large numbers operates and applies to insurance.

Key Words and Phrases

Law of large numbers (p. 1.5)

Exposure unit (p. 1.5)

Review Questions

3-1. Explain how exposure units can be independent of each other. (p. 1.5)

3-2. Give an example of an exposure unit. (p. 1.5)

3-3. How are insurers able to accurately predict the number of losses they might incur? (p. 1.5)

Application Question

3-4. In a large corporation's pool of 10,000 automobiles, the corporation experiences losses to vehicles ranging from 5 percent to 15 percent in any given year. In a small company with 50 automobiles, the company experiences losses to vehicles ranging from 0 percent to 50 percent in any given year. How do these results reinforce the concept of the law of large numbers? (p. 1.5)

Educational Objective 4
Describe the major types of loss exposures.

Key Words and Phrases

Property loss exposure (p. 1.6)

Real property (p. 1.6)

Personal property (p. 1.6)

Net income (p. 1.6)

Net income loss (p. 1.6)

Liability loss exposure (p. 1.6)

Liability loss (p. 1.7)

Personal loss exposure (p. 1.7)

Personnel loss exposure (p. 1.7)

Review Questions

4-1. Categorize each of the following as a property, liability, personal, or personnel loss exposure. (pp. 1.5–1.7)

   a. The possibility that your neighbor would sue you for damage done by your dog to her property.

   b. The possibility that your wallet could be stolen.

1.8 Property and Liability Insurance Principles—INS 21

    c. The possibility faced by a movie producer that the actress playing the main character would die before completing the movie.

    d. The possibility that you would become injured and unable to earn an income.

4-2. Give an example of real and personal property that a business owner may possess. (p. 1.6)

4-3. What causes a net income loss? (p. 1.6)

Application Question

4-4. In a single fire that started in its boiler room, a manufacturer experienced losses to its building and inventory. Two workers were injured as they escaped the building. In addition, the heat from the fire damaged two neighboring buildings and made them unusable for a period of two weeks. Explain how this single loss demonstrates the three major types of loss exposures. (pp. 1.5–1.7)

Educational Objective 5
Describe the characteristics of an ideally insurable loss exposure.

Review Questions

5-1. Insurers generally prefer to provide insurance for loss exposures that have certain characteristics. Using an example, explain why each of the following characteristics of a loss exposure tends to make it possible to provide insurance. (pp. 1.8–1.10)

   a. Losses that involve pure risk

   b. Losses that are accidental

c. Losses that are definite and measurable

d. Large number of similar exposure units

e. Losses that are not catastrophic

f. Loss exposures that are economically feasible to insure

5-2. Loss exposures must be definite and measurable to be insurable. (p. 1.8)

a. Give an example of an occurrence that could be insured.

b. Give an example of an occurrence that could *not* be insured.

5-3. Explain how an insurer can offer windstorm coverage and avoid the financial difficulty that a major windstorm can cause. (p. 1.9)

Application Question

5-4. Grocery Store is a chain of 100 large grocery stores. Annually, Grocery Store receives 500 complaints regarding dents that customers receive on their vehicles from grocery carts in the parking lot. The grocery carts are used carelessly by customers who allow them to roll into vehicles in the parking lot, causing scratches and dents. The average damage for each loss is $75. Do these losses exhibit the characteristics of an ideally insurable loss exposure? (pp. 1.7–1.10)

Educational Objective 6

Explain why government insurance is needed, and give examples of federal insurance programs and state insurance programs.

Review Questions

6-1. In addition to private insurers, what other entities provide insurance? (p. 1.11)

6-2. Why do federal and state government insurance programs exist? (pp. 1.11–1.12)

6-3. Briefly describe at least two federal government insurance programs. (p. 1.11)

6-4. Briefly describe at least two state government insurance programs. (p. 1.12)

Insurance: What Is It? 1.13

Application Question

6-5. Social Security is a federal government program that (among other benefits) provides a base-level income to beneficiaries who reach the age at which they can collect benefits. Justify the need for this program to be administered by the federal government. (p. 1.11)

Educational Objective 7

Describe the major business operations of insurers.

Review Questions

7-1. Briefly explain the purpose of each of the following insurance operations. (pp. 1.12–1.13)

   a. Marketing

   b. Underwriting

   c. Claim handling

d. Ratemaking

7-2. Explain how each of the following representatives plays a part in insurer operations. (pp. 1.12–1.13)

a. Insurance producers involved in marketing insurance

b. Underwriters

c. Claim representatives

7-3. Why do insurers make investments? (p. 1.13)

Insurance: What Is It?

7-4. Why do insurers use ratemaking to establish appropriate insurance rates? (p. 1.13)

Application Questions

7-5. The homeowners in a community have formed an association. Each homeowner pays $20 per month for the upkeep of the fence surrounding the community and the landscaping in the commonly shared areas. What type of private insurer does this association most closely resemble? (p. 1.11)

7-6. An insurer's financial results deteriorated last year because of a large number of forest fires that swept through California and destroyed homes concentrated in neighborhoods bordering forested areas. What department is responsible for ensuring that the insurer does not experience similar results in subsequent years? (p. 1.13)

Educational Objective 8

Explain why and how state insurance departments regulate insurers.

Review Questions

8-1. Why do state insurance departments monitor the financial condition of insurers? (p. 1.14)

8-2. Why do state insurance departments regulate insurance rates? (p. 1.14)

8-3. Identify three ways in which state insurance departments regulate insurers. (p. 1.15)

Insurance: What Is It? 1.17

Application Question

8-4. The insurers doing business in a state implemented sharp increases in rates following a hurricane that caused extensive losses in that state. The insurers stated that they were recouping the funds for the losses that they experienced. How are the policyholders protected from rates that exceed reasonable increases? (p. 1.14)

Educational Objective 9
Describe the benefits of insurance.

Key Word or Phrase
Indemnify (p. 1.15)

Review Questions

9-1. How does the business of insurance benefit individuals, families, businesses, and society as a whole in each of the following ways? (pp. 1.15–1.17)

   a. Payment for losses

   b. Reduction of uncertainty

c. Loss control activities

d. More efficient use of resources

e. Support for credit

f. Satisfaction of legal requirements

g. Satisfaction of business requirements

h. Source of investment funds

i. Reduction of social burdens

9-2. Explain how insurance practically eliminates an insured's uncertainty about financial consequences of a loss. (p. 1.16)

9-3. After learning that you decided to take an insurance course, your friend Helen said that, in her opinion, the world would be a better place without insurance. What benefits of insurance make the world a better place? (pp. 1.15–1.17)

Application Question

9-4. Many auto owners feel that they are safe drivers and have no need for purchasing automobile insurance. They complain that they have purchased coverage for years and have never made a claim against their policy. They state that they could have saved the premiums over the years, placed the money in a savings account, and paid for any losses. Justify the need for automobile insurance, even if a policyholder has never experienced a claim. (pp. 1.15–1.17)

Educational Objective 10

Describe the costs of insurance.

Review Questions

10-1. Why must insurers receive more money in premiums and investment income than they pay in losses? (p. 1.18)

10-2. What operating expenses add to the cost of insurance? (p. 1.18)

10-3. Money and other resources not spent on insurance could instead be used in another activity. What is the term for this category of costs? (p. 1.18)

10-4. How may insurance actually encourage losses? (pp. 1.18–1.19)

10-5. Why may insurance increase the number of lawsuits? (p. 1.19)

Application Question

10-6. John strained his back while lifting a large box while at work. Following some physical therapy and rest, John was fully restored and free from pain. John claimed that the pain continued so that he could have an additional four weeks of disability coverage and an extended vacation. Explain how John's behavior is a cost of insurance. (pp. 1.18–1.19)

Educational Objective 11
Distinguish among the major types of property and liability insurance.

Key Words and Phrases
Fire and allied lines insurance (p. 1.21)

Business income insurance, or business interruption insurance (p. 1.21)

Crime insurance (p. 1.21)

Ocean marine insurance (p. 1.21)

Inland marine insurance (p. 1.21)

Auto physical damage insurance (p. 1.21)

Auto liability insurance (p. 1.22)

Commercial general liability insurance (p. 1.22)

Personal liability insurance (p. 1.22)

Professional liability insurance (p. 1.22)

Review Questions

11-1. For what two types of loss exposures does property insurance provide protection? (p. 1.20)

11-2. Using examples, explain why the head of a family would probably purchase each of the following types of insurance. (pp. 1.20–1.22)

   a. Property insurance

   b. Liability insurance

11-3. Distinguish between the parties involved in property insurance and those who are involved in liability insurance. (pp. 1.21–1.22)

Educational Objective 12
Distinguish among the major types of life and health insurance.

Key Words and Phrases

Whole life insurance (p. 1.23)

Cash value (p. 1.23)

Term insurance (p. 1.23)

Universal life insurance (p. 1.23)

Medical insurance (p. 1.23)

Disability income insurance (p. 1.24)

Review Questions

12-1. Why would someone purchase term life insurance instead of whole life insurance? (p. 1.23)

12-2. Using examples, explain why the head of the family would probably purchase each of the following types of insurance. (pp. 1.23–1.24)

　a. Life insurance

　b. Health insurance

12-3. Explain how medical insurance differs from disability insurance. (pp. 1.23–1.24)

Application Questions

12-4. Because she owns and operates an auto, Mary faces some loss exposures. Therefore, she buys auto liability and physical damage insurance from Atwell Insurance Company. (Educational Objectives 1, 2, 3, and 4)

　a. What loss exposures does Mary face?

b. How has Mary transferred her auto-related losses to Atwell?

c. By buying insurance, how is Mary sharing the costs of her possible auto-related losses with other insurance buyers?

d. Mary will pay a few hundred dollars in premium, but Atwell might pay thousands of dollars if she has an accident. How can Atwell afford to do this?

12-5. Although some private insurers participate in the National Flood Insurance Program sponsored by the federal government, flood insurance on real property is not directly provided by private insurers because the flood loss exposure does not have the characteristics of an ideally insurable loss exposure. (Educational Objectives 5 and 6)

   a. What are the characteristics of an ideally insurable loss exposure?

   b. Explain which characteristics of an ideally insurable loss exposure are not met by the flood loss exposure.

Answers to Assignment 1 Questions

NOTE: These answers are provided to give students a basic understanding of acceptable types of responses. They often are not the only valid answers and are not intended to provide an exhaustive response to the questions.

Educational Objective 1

1-1. To manage risk, persons or organizations may use retention, avoidance, loss prevention and loss reduction measures, or loss transfer.

Educational Objective 2

2-1. Insurance is described as a transfer system because it transfers the costs of losses from a person, a family, or a business to an insurer. The insurer, in turn, pays for covered losses and, in effect, distributes the costs of losses among all insureds. Therefore, insurance is a system of both transferring and sharing the cost of losses.

2-2. Insurance buyers can transfer the costs of their losses to insurers by buying insurance.

2-3. Insurance spreads the cost of losses among all insureds by pooling the premiums paid by all insureds and using the money to pay covered losses.

2-4. The threat of loss to any single colonist is transferred to the entire group of colonists. The cost of loss to any home is shared by the entire community. This arrangement is similar to insurance, which distributes the cost of losses among all insureds.

Educational Objective 3

3-1. Exposure units can be independent of each other if they are not subject to the same event.

3-2. An example of an exposure unit in property insurance is a car or a house.

3-3. Insurers can accurately predict the number of losses they might incur because of the large number of independent exposure units (the cars and houses of all their insureds, for example). Using that number, they can predict the number of losses that all similar exposure units combined are likely to experience.

3-4. As the number of similar but independent exposure units increases, the relative accuracy of predictions about future outcomes also increases. In this case, the large corporation's results are more predictable. In contrast, the smaller company's results are less predictable as evidenced by the larger range of losses.

Educational Objective 4

4-1. a. The possibility that a neighbor would sue you for damage done by your dog to her property would be categorized as a liability loss exposure.

b. The possibility that an individual's wallet could be stolen would be categorized as a property loss exposure.

c. The possibility faced by a movie producer that the actress playing the main character would die before completing the movie would be categorized as a personnel loss exposure.

d. The possibility that you would become injured and unable to earn an income would be categorized as a personal loss exposure.

4-2. Examples of real property that a business owner may possess are a factory building or the land on which it is situated. Examples of personal property a business owner may possess are the equipment and machinery in a factory building or the inventory of a retail merchant.

4-3. A net income loss is the result of a reduction in revenue, an increase in expenses, or both.

4-4. The single loss from the fire has resulted in losses that cover the three major loss exposures:
- The loss to the building and inventory are property losses.
- The loss to the neighboring buildings and their use are liability losses.
- The injury to the workers is a personnel loss.

Educational Objective 5

5-1. The type of insurance selected for discussion is auto liability coverage. The characteristics of auto liability coverage that make it an ideally insurable loss exposure include the following:
  a. It involves pure risk because there is no possibility of gain.
  b. Losses are accidental; therefore, the insured generally has no incentive to cause an intentional auto liability loss to a third party.
  c. Losses are definite and measurable, such as costs to repair or replace damage to a car and the cost of medical expenses.
  d. Because most drivers need auto coverage, there are a large number of similar exposure units.
  e. Losses are not catastrophic. Auto liability losses are independent—a liability loss suffered by one insured does not generally affect any other insureds.
  f. Losses are economically feasible to insure because an auto liability loss has a low probability of occurrence as well as the potential for high severity.

5-2. a. An example of an occurrence that could be insured would be the sudden bursting of a water pipe that causes water damage in the insured's bathroom.
  b. An example of an occurrence that could not be insured would be a slow leak in a bathroom pipe that causes decay and rotting of the insured's floor over several years.

5-3. An insurer can offer windstorm coverage and avoid the financial difficulty that a major windstorm can cause by diversifying the homes and businesses it insures so that it does not have a heavy concentration of insureds in any one geographical area.

5-4. To answer the question, you must compare Grocery Store's loss exposure to the characteristics of an ideally insurable loss exposure:
- Pure, not speculative risk: There is a possibility of a loss or no loss, but no possibility of gain.
- Similar exposure units: Yes, the loss exposures appear to be similar.
- Accidental: From Grocery Store's perspective, the losses are accidental in nature.
- Definite and measurable: Yes, the losses are definite in time and have measurable outcomes.
- Not catastrophic: The losses are not catastrophic in nature.
- Economically feasible to insure: The losses are relatively small and are highly probable. For this reason, this is probably not an ideally insurable loss exposure.

Educational Objective 6

6-1. In addition to private insurers, federal and state governments provide insurance.

6-2. The federal insurance programs exist because the government has huge financial resources for providing certain types of coverage and has the authority to require mandatory coverage in some cases. The state government insurance programs exist because the state can ensure the availability of coverage considered necessary to protect the public by operating insurance plans for insureds who have difficulty obtaining insurance from private insurers.

6-3.
- The National Flood Insurance Program is a federal government insurance program that provides insurance for owners of property located in flood-prone areas and for others concerned about the exposure of flooding.
- The Federal Crop Insurance Program is a federal government insurance program that insures farmers against damage to their crops by drought, insects, hail, and other causes.

6-4.
- Fair Access to Insurance Requirements (FAIR) plans are state government insurance programs that provide basic property insurance to property owners who cannot otherwise obtain needed coverage.
- Automobile insurance plans are state government insurance plans that make auto insurance available to drivers who have difficulty obtaining insurance from private insurers.

6-5. The extent of the coverage provided by Social Security and its mandatory nature could not be supported by a private insurer. A program this large in scope can only be insured federally.

Educational Objective 7

7-1.
a. The purpose of the marketing insurance operation is to determine customers' needs and sell and deliver insurance products or services to them.
b. The purpose of the underwriting insurance operation is to decide which potential customers to insure and what coverage to offer them.
c. The purpose of the claim handling insurance operation is to determine whether a covered loss has occurred and, if so, the amount to be paid for the loss.
d. The purpose of the ratemaking insurance operation is to determine the rates to charge for each category of insureds.

7-2.
a. Insurance producers involved in marketing insurance play a part in insurer operations in that they represent insurers in selling and delivering insurance products to the public.
b. Underwriters play a part in insurer operations in that they select insureds, price coverage, and determine policy terms and conditions.
c. Claim representatives play a part in insurer operations in that they satisfy the insurer's obligations under an insurance policy by promptly responding to claims and gathering the information necessary to evaluate a claim properly and reach a fair settlement.

7-3. Insurers make investments because they receive premiums before they pay for losses and expenses. Consequently, insurers can generate investment income by investing these premiums prudently.

7-4. Insurers need appropriate rates to have enough money to pay for losses, cover operating expenses, and earn a reasonable profit.

7-5. The homeowners association resembles a mutual insurer in which the organization is owned by the policyholders.

7-6. The underwriting department decides which potential customers to insure and prices the coverage. This department must make adjustments in insured selection or pricing to prevent similar financial results in the future.

Educational Objective 8

8-1. State insurance departments monitor the financial condition of insurers because a weak insurer may not have the resources necessary to meet its obligations.

8-2. State insurance departments regulate insurance rates to protect consumers from inadequate, excessive, or unfairly discriminatory rates.

8-3. State insurance departments regulate insurers in the following three ways:
  (1) They require that insurers file their policy forms so that the department can approve policy language.
  (2) They monitor specific insurer practices concerning marketing, underwriting, and claims.
  (3) They investigate complaints against insurers and their representatives and enforce standards regarding their conduct.

8-4. Each state has an insurance department that ensures that rates are adequate, are not excessive, and are not unfairly discriminatory. The state insurance department will review the rates charged for the consumers' protection.

Educational Objective 9

9-1. a. The business of insurance benefits individuals, families, businesses, and society with payment for losses by indemnifying individuals for covered losses.
  b. The business of insurance benefits individuals, families, businesses, and society with reduction of uncertainty by transferring the financial consequences of an accidental loss from the insured to the insurer.
  c. The business of insurance benefits individuals, families, businesses, and society with loss control activities by recommending loss control practices that reduce insured losses, thereby keeping down insurance costs.
  d. The business of insurance benefits individuals, families, businesses, and society by making more efficient use of resources because it is unnecessary to set aside a large amount of money to pay for the financial consequences of loss exposures that can be insured and frees up funds for other uses.
  e. The business of insurance benefits individuals, families, businesses, and society with support for credit by reducing the lender's uncertainty by guaranteeing that the lender will be paid if the collateral for the loan is destroyed or damaged by an insured event.
  f. The business of insurance benefits individuals, families, businesses, and society by meeting some legal obligations, like employers' obligations to provide workers' compensation benefits.
  g. The business of insurance benefits individuals, families, businesses, and society by satisfying some business requirements, such as providing a building contractor's requirement of proof of insurance.

h. The business of insurance benefits individuals, families, businesses, and society as a source of investment funds by using the invested money for projects such as new construction, research, and technology.

i. The business of insurance benefits individuals, families, businesses, and society in the reduction of social burdens by providing compensation to injured persons who might otherwise use state welfare funds or the assistance of another social program.

9-2. Insurance practically eliminates an insured's uncertainty about financial consequences of a loss because the uncertainty is transferred to an insurer. Insurers have greater certainty than individuals about losses because the law of large numbers enables insurers to predict the number of losses that are likely to occur and the financial effects of those losses.

9-3. Insurance makes the world a better place because it provides the following:
- Recommendations for loss control activities
- Support for credit
- Satisfaction of legal requirements
- Satisfaction of business requirements
- A source of investment funds
- A reduction of social burdens

9-4.
- Automobile insurance will indemnify losses to others that auto owners may cause. The amount of potential losses may exceed what auto owners can afford to pay. Such losses can financially devastate auto owners.
- Automobile insurance coverage reduces the uncertainty of loss. Insured auto owners are exchanging a small known premium amount for a potentially large unknown loss.
- Rather than saving money for an unknown loss, auto owners can make more efficient use of their resources.
- Automobile policies satisfy state proof of insurance requirements.
- Insurance coverage will cover losses caused to innocent third parties, thereby reducing the burden to society in caring for these victims.

Educational Objective 10

10-1. Insurers need to receive more money in premiums and investment income than they pay in losses to pay for losses and for the costs of doing business.

10-2. The following operating expenses add to the cost of insurance:
- Salaries
- Producers' commissions
- Advertising
- Building expenses
- Equipment
- Taxes
- Licensing fees

10-3. Opportunity costs are the money and other resources used in the business of insurance that could have been used in another activity.

10-4. Insurance may encourage losses, such as in the following example: An insured intentionally causes a loss by committing arson or exaggerates a loss that has occurred by inflating a claim, because insurance is available to pay for losses that occur. Other insureds may not be as careful as they would be without insurance or may not try to prevent losses.

10-5. One reason insurance could increase the number of lawsuits is that liability insurers often pay large sums of money to persons who have been injured. Some people may view liability insurance as a pool of money available to anyone who has suffered injury or damage, with little regard given to fault.

10-6. John has an incentive in the form of a vacation with income to delay his return to work. This is a cost of insurance (in this case a deliberate cost) that is shared by everyone who purchases insurance.

Educational Objective 11

11-1. Property insurance provides coverage for property and net income loss exposures.

11-2. a. A head of a family may purchase property insurance to pay the cost to replace personal property that a burglar steals from the insured's house.
b. A head of a family may purchase liability insurance to pay the cost to repair or to replace a parked car that the insured's car collides with.

11-3. Two parties are involved in property insurance: the insured and the insurer. Liability insurance differs in that three parties are involved in a liability loss: the insured, the insurer, and the party who is injured or whose property is damaged by the insured. This is why liability insurance is sometimes called "third-party insurance."

Educational Objective 12

12-1. Someone would purchase term life insurance if the person wanted coverage for a specified time period. Also, someone might purchase term life insurance instead of whole life insurance if the person had no desire to borrow from the cash value that accumulates in a whole life policy or if the person wanted the maximum amount of life insurance protection available at the lowest cost.

12-2. a. A head of a family may purchase life insurance to pay expenses related to an insured's death, such as a funeral.
b. A head of a family may purchase health insurance to reimburse the insured's costs of medical expenses for surgery, such as hospital costs and doctor's fees.

12-3. Medical insurance differs from disability insurance in that the former covers medical expenses that result from illness or injury. Disability insurance provides periodic income payments to an insured who is unable to work as a result of an accident or sickness. Disability insurance is primarily income replacement insurance that pays weekly or monthly benefits until the insured can return to work or until a maximum period has elapsed.

12-4. a. Loss exposures that Mary faces because she owns and operates an auto are: her car could be damaged or destroyed; she or her passengers could be injured in an accident; and, if she causes an accident, she might become responsible for injury or damage to others or their property.

b. Mary has transferred her auto-related losses to Atwell by exchanging a comparatively small premium for an agreement by Atwell to pay even large losses that are covered by the insurance contract.

c. In purchasing insurance, Mary is sharing the costs of her possible auto-related losses with other insurance buyers, because many insurance buyers will pay a premium, but only some of them will have losses. All insurance buyers are indirectly providing the funds that are used to pay claims; therefore, they really share the costs of each other's losses.

d. Atwell can afford to pay more for a claim than it receives from an insured's premium because the company will collect premiums from other insureds who do not have an accident. The law of large numbers helps the insurer predict its losses so it can collect enough premiums to fund them all.

12-5. a. The characteristics of an ideally insurable loss exposure are as follows:
- Loss exposures that involve pure, not speculative risk
- Large number of similar, but independent, exposures
- Losses that are accidental
- Losses that are definite and measurable
- Losses that are not catastrophic
- Losses that are economically feasible to insure

b. The flood exposure does not meet the characteristics of an ideally insurable loss exposure for the following reasons:
- Flood losses can be catastrophic and exposure units in a geographical area are not independent. A single flood could cause losses to a sizable proportion of insureds at the same time.
- Flood exposures with a high probability of loss are not economically feasible to insure.

Direct Your Learning

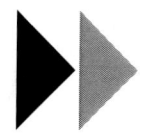

ASSIGNMENT 2

Who Provides Insurance and How Is It Regulated?

Educational Objectives

After learning the content of this assignment, you should be able to:

1. Describe the various types of private insurers that provide property-casualty insurance:
   a. Stock insurers
   b. Mutual insurers
   c. Reciprocal insurance exchanges
   d. Lloyd's
   e. American Lloyds
   f. Captive insurers
   g. Reinsurance companies
2. Describe the federal government Social Security program.
3. Identify other federal insurance programs.
4. Describe common state government insurance programs:
   a. Workers' compensation insurance funds
   b. Unemployment insurance programs
   c. Automobile insurance plans
   d. Fair Access to Insurance Requirements (FAIR) plans
   e. Beachfront and windstorm pools
   f. Insurance guarantee funds
5. Describe the purpose and activities of the National Association of Insurance Commissioners (NAIC).
6. Explain how insurance rates are developed.
7. Describe the objectives of rate regulation.
8. Describe the different types of insurance rating laws.
9. Explain how insurance regulators monitor insurers' financial condition and protect consumers.
10. Explain how the excess and surplus lines market meets the needs of various classes of business that are often unable to find insurance in the standard market.
11. Summarize the historical and present-day effect on insurance regulation of the following court decisions, legislation passed, and legislation under review:
    a. U.S. Supreme Court decision in the *South-Eastern Underwriters Association* case
    b. McCarran-Ferguson Act
    c. Gramm-Leach-Bliley Act
    d. State Modernization and Regulatory Transparency Act (SMART Act)
12. Define or describe each of the Key Words and Phrases for this assignment.

Study Materials

Required Reading:
- Property and Liability Insurance Principles
  - Chapter 2
- "State Versus Federal Regulation of Insurance—A Changing Landscape," Course Guide Reading 2-1

Study Aids:
- SMART Online Practice Exams
- SMART Study Aids
  - Review Notes and Flash Cards—Assignment 2

Outline

- **Types of Insurance Organizations**
  - A. Private Insurers
    1. Stock Insurers
    2. Mutual Insurers
    3. Reciprocal Insurance Exchanges
    4. Lloyd's
    5. American Lloyds
    6. Captive Insurers
    7. Reinsurance Companies
  - B. Government Insurance Programs
    1. Federal Government Insurance Programs
    2. State Government Insurance Programs
- **Insurance Regulation**
  - A. National Association of Insurance Commissioners (NAIC)
  - B. Rate Regulation
    1. Ratemaking
    2. Objectives of Rate Regulation
    3. Insurance Rating Laws
  - C. Solvency Surveillance
    1. Insurer Examinations
    2. Insurance Regulatory Information System (IRIS)
  - D. Consumer Protection
    1. Licensing Insurers
    2. Licensing Insurer Representatives
    3. Approving Policy Forms
    4. Examining Market Conduct
    5. Investigating Consumer Complaints
- **Excess and Surplus Lines Insurance**
  - A. Classes of E&S Business
    1. Unusual or Unique Loss Exposures
    2. Nonstandard Business
    3. Insureds Needing High Limits of Coverage
    4. Insureds Needing Unusually Broad Coverage
    5. Loss Exposures That Require New Forms
  - B. Excess and Surplus Lines Regulation
- **Summary**
- **"State Versus Federal Regulation of Insurance—A Changing Landscape" (Course Guide Reading 2-1)**

s.m.a.r.t. tips

Reduce the number of Key Words and Phrases that you must review. SMART Flash Cards contain the Key Words and Phrases and their definitions, allowing you to set aside those cards that you have mastered.

Reading 2-1

State Versus Federal Regulation of Insurance— A Changing Landscape

by Robert H. Zetterstrom, Esq., CPCU

The status of "state versus federal regulation of the insurance industry" is in flux. Convergent forces are operating that will likely change the existing landscape where insurance companies are first and foremost regulated by individual states.

To understand these forces, one must return to June 5, 1944, when Justice Black delivered the opinion of a divided United States Supreme Court in the *U.S. v. South-Eastern Underwriters Association* case (*SEUA*). The court held for the first time that insurers conducting their activities across state lines are within the regulatory power of Congress under the commerce clause of the U.S. Constitution. A prior decision in *Paul v. Virginia* held that the business of insurance was not the transaction of commerce within federal antitrust laws. In the *SEUA* case, the court upheld an indictment brought by the federal government under Sections 1 and 2 of the Sherman Antitrust Act. Various insurance companies were indicted for fixing and maintaining arbitrary and non-competitive rates on fire and specified allied lines of insurance as well as monopolizing trade among the states of Alabama, Florida, Georgia, North Carolina, South Carolina and Virginia. The *SEUA* decision opened the door for the option of federal regulation of the insurance industry.

Congress quickly moved to close the door by reversing the *SEUA* decision through passage of the McCarran-Ferguson Act, so that insurers would be generally exempt from federal antitrust laws. The McCarran-Ferguson Act provides, in part, that the Sherman Antitrust Act "shall be applicable to the business of insurance to the extent that such business is not regulated by state law." The enactment of the McCarran-Ferguson Act has largely left the regulation of insurance companies to the individual states ever since its passage.

Lately, Congress has been moving in a direction toward retaking some of the power to regulate insurers that it relinquished in passing the McCarran-Ferguson Act. In 1999, the Gramm-Leach-Bliley Act (GLB) was passed which represented financial services reform. GLB created new opportunities for financial services organizations by allowing companies to offer bank, insurance, and securities products within the same corporate structure. One provision of GLB created pressure on state legislatures to adopt uniform insurance producer licensing laws or face the creation of a national producer licensing quasi-governmental agency entitled the National Association of Registered Agents and Brokers (NARAB). The threat of a national licensing system caused the states to adopt uniform licensing laws so NARAB was never formed.

GLB, while promoting uniform producer licensing laws, did reaffirm the McCarran-Ferguson Act. GLB was an attempt to reconcile federal banking and security laws with a state regulatory system for the insurance industry. GLB provides a framework to determine what financial products are banking or security products subject to federal oversight and what products are insurance products regulated at the state level. The concept of "functional regulation" was born in GLB. The Senate committee enacting GLB stated: "Accordingly, the bill is intended to ensure that banking activities are regulated by bank regulators, securities activities are regulated by securities regulators and insurance activities are regulated by insurance regulators." It should be noted that the McCarran-Ferguson Act does not always mandate state law supremacy over federal law to regulate insurance. Federal law may preempt state law if the state law does not relate to the regulation or taxation of insurance or the federal law specifically relates to the business of insurance.

A bill titled the State Modernization and Regulatory Transparency Act (SMART Act) is being considered for enactment into law by the House Financial Securities Committee. The SMART Act would impose uniform standards across a wide array of insurance regulatory issues including producer licensing, life and property-casualty insurance, surplus lines, reinsurance, market conduct, anti-fraud, and others. The most controversial area of the SMART Act is its preemption of state regulation of insurance rates.

The SMART Act would not create federal regulations or provide for federal licenses for insurers. The Act, if passed, would however dramatically affect how states regulate insurance companies because states would be required to apply uniform provisions. Functional regulation would be maintained in that the states would continue to regulate insurers; however, the SMART Act would mandate to the state how that regulation should be done.

Congress is also examining the enforcement of antitrust laws through the Antitrust Modernization Commission. This commission is mandated to study whether various industry exemptions and immunities, including McCarran-Ferguson, should be continued. Upon completion of its study, a report is to be filed with Congress and the President by April 2007. The Commission may suggest a completely different approach to the regulation of insurance than that envisioned by the SMART Act.

In January 2005, Marsh & McLennan, the largest insurance brokerage in the U.S., settled a suit filed by Eliot Spitzer, the New York Attorney General. The settlement was reported to be $850 million. The suit involved alleged improprieties in payment of producer compensation. There have been a number of reactions to the New York Attorney General's investigation. Each state around the country is assessing what regulatory response is appropriate, and a number of states have begun their own investigations. How these investigations are resolved may have a profound influence on whether Congress adopts the SMART Act approach (creating uniform standards to be enforced by individual states) or the repeal of the McCarran-Ferguson Act (creating the opportunity for direct federal regulation of the insurance industry).

The only thing that appears certain at this time is that some change in the existing regulatory landscape will occur. Stay tuned.

Who Provides Insurance and How Is It Regulated? 2.5

For each assignment, you should define or describe each of the Key Words and Phrases and answer each of the Review and Application Questions.

Educational Objective 1

Describe the various types of private insurers that provide property-casualty insurance:

a. Stock insurers
b. Mutual insurers
c. Reciprocal insurance exchanges
d. Lloyd's
e. American Lloyds
f. Captive insurers
g. Reinsurance companies

Key Words and Phrases

Stock insurer (p. 2.4)

Mutual insurer (p. 2.6)

Demutualization (p. 2.6)

Reciprocal insurance exchange, or interinsurance exchange (p. 2.6)

Subscribers (p. 2.6)

Attorney-in-fact (p. 2.7)

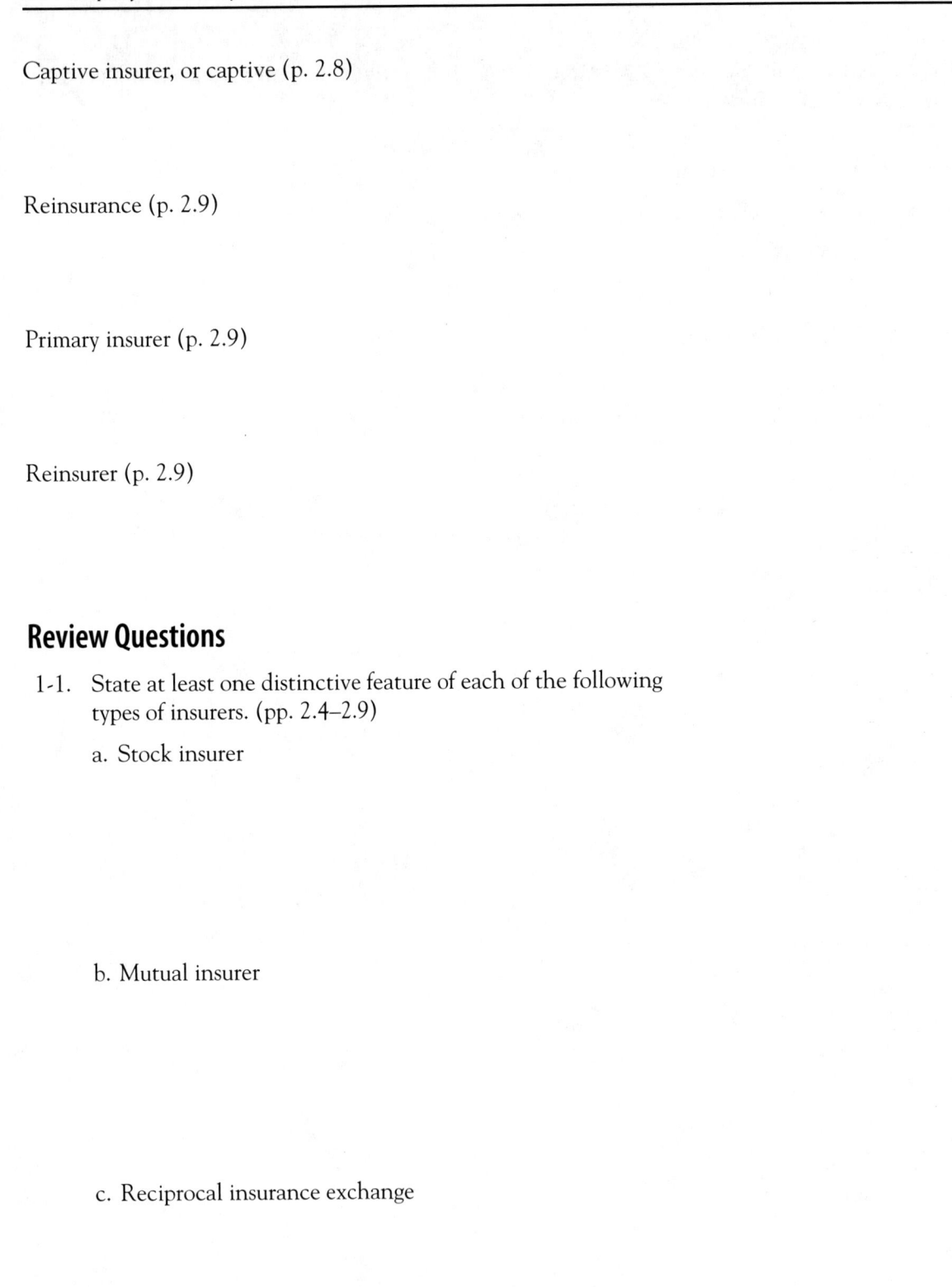

2.6 Property and Liability Insurance Principles—INS 21

Captive insurer, or captive (p. 2.8)

Reinsurance (p. 2.9)

Primary insurer (p. 2.9)

Reinsurer (p. 2.9)

Review Questions

1-1. State at least one distinctive feature of each of the following types of insurers. (pp. 2.4–2.9)

    a. Stock insurer

    b. Mutual insurer

    c. Reciprocal insurance exchange

d. Lloyd's

e. American Lloyds

f. Captive insurer

g. Reinsurance company

1-2. What are three reasons why some corporations use a captive insurer? (pp. 2.8–2.9)

1-3. What are two reasons why insurers buy reinsurance? (p. 2.9)

Educational Objective 2
Describe the federal government Social Security program.

Review Questions

2-1. Provide an example of how some federal insurance programs serve the public in a manner that only the government can. (p. 2.10)

2-2. Briefly describe the Social Security program. (p. 2.10)

2-3. Explain why the federal government is involved in the Social Security program. (p. 2.10)

Educational Objective 3

Identify other federal insurance programs.

Review Question

3-1. Identify two federal insurance programs. (p. 2.10)

Application Question

3-2. Pharmaceutical companies are concerned about the possible harmful side effects that can occur when they release a new drug. Considering the types of loss exposures that the federal government insures, speculate whether the federal government would be likely to provide insurance for this liability coverage for the pharmaceutical industry. (p. 2.10)

> ### Educational Objective 4
> Describe common state government insurance programs:
> a. Workers' compensation insurance funds
> b. Unemployment insurance programs
> c. Automobile insurance plans
> d. Fair Access to Insurance Requirements (FAIR) plans
> e. Beachfront and windstorm pools
> f. Insurance guarantee funds

Key Words and Phrases

Monopolistic state fund (p. 2.11)

Competitive state fund (p. 2.11)

Residual market plan, or shared market plan (p. 2.11)

Guaranty fund (p. 2.12)

Review Questions

4-1. Briefly describe three state insurance programs. (pp. 2.10–2.12)

4-2. What are the three types of state workers' compensation insurance funds? (p. 2.11)

4-3. How do insurance guaranty funds operate to protect policyholders? (p. 2.12)

Application Question

4-4. FAIR plans and beachfront and windstorm insurance pools are organized and managed on a state, rather than a federal, basis. Applying your knowledge of these state insurance programs, discuss why it is appropriate that they are managed by individual states. (p. 2.12)

Educational Objective 5
Describe the purpose and activities of the National Association of Insurance Commissioners (NAIC).

Key Words and Phrases
National Association of Insurance Commissioners (NAIC) (p. 2.13)

Model law (p. 2.13)

Review Questions

5-1. Who are the members of the National Association of Insurance Commissioners (NAIC)? (p. 2.13)

5-2. What does the National Association of Insurance Commissioners do that encourages coordination and cooperation among state insurance departments? (pp. 2.13–2.14)

5-3. What are the three primary objectives of insurance regulation? (p. 2.13)

Application Question

5-4. The model laws created by the NAIC are not mandated. Rather, they are proposed statutes that each state legislature considers for possible enactment. Explain why it would be beneficial for each state to have the flexibility of adopting, changing, or rejecting the model laws rather than making them mandatory for each state. (p. 2.13)

Educational Objective 6
Explain how insurance rates are developed.

Key Words and Phrases

Ratemaking (p. 2.14)

Rate (p. 2.14)

Premium (p. 2.14)

Actuary (p. 2.15)

Review Questions

6-1. In your own words, clearly explain the difference between rates and premiums. (p. 2.14)

6-2. Explain how insurers determine the premiums to charge. (p. 2.15)

6-3. How do insurers use rate classification systems to differentiate among insureds? (p. 2.15)

Application Question

6-4. Insurance rates are developed to reflect each insured's share of predicted losses. If two automobiles of the same make, model, and year are insured by the same insurer for the same limit of coverage, what may account for differences in the premiums charged for coverage on the two vehicles? (pp. 2.14–2.15)

Educational Objective 7

Describe the objectives of rate regulation.

Key Words and Phrases

Actuarial equity (p. 2.16)

Social equity (p. 2.16)

Unfair discrimination (p. 2.17)

Review Questions

7-1. What are the three objectives of rate regulation? (p. 2.15)

7-2. Explain why the goal of rate adequacy conflicts with pressures to hold down insurance premiums. (p. 2.16)

7-3. Historically, young male drivers have had worse auto accident records than young female drivers. Should young male drivers pay more for their auto insurance? Explain how both actuarial equity and social equity concepts may be applied in answering this question. (p. 2.16)

Application Question

7-4. Homeowners insurance rates are different for frame and brick houses. Brick houses are charged a lower premium. It could be argued that brick houses are not substantially different from frame houses: they are usually only a frame house with a veneer of brick covering the exterior. If this could be proven, how would the objectives of rate regulation respond? (p. 2.17)

Educational Objective 8
Describe the different types of insurance rating laws.

Key Words and Phrases

Prior-approval law (p. 2.17)

Flex rating law (p. 2.17)

File-and-use law (p. 2.17)

Use-and-file law (p. 2.17)

Open competition, or no-file law (p. 2.17)

State-mandated rates (p. 2.17)

Exempt commercial policyholders (p. 2.18)

Non-filed inland marine (p. 2.18)

Review Questions

8-1. List and give a brief explanation of the six primary categories of insurance rating laws. (p. 2.17)

8-2. Briefly describe the three broad exceptions to typical rating laws. (p. 2.18)

> **Educational Objective 9**
> Explain how insurance regulators monitor insurers' financial condition and protect consumers.

Key Words and Phrases

Solvency (p. 2.18)

Solvency surveillance (p. 2.18)

Insurance Regulatory Information System (IRIS) (p. 2.19)

Licensed insurer, or admitted insurer (p. 2.19)

Domestic insurer (p. 2.19)

Foreign insurer (p. 2.19)

Alien insurer (p. 2.19)

Market conduct regulation (p. 2.21)

Review Questions

9-1. How do insurance regulators monitor the solvency of insurers doing business in their states? (pp. 2.18–2.19)

9-2. How does each of the following insurance regulatory activities serve to protect insurance consumers? (pp. 2.19–2.21)

   a. Licensing insurers

   b. Licensing insurer representatives

   c. Approving policy forms

   d. Examining market conduct

e. Investigating consumer complaints

9-3. Explain what action state regulators take if an insurer fails to meet financial standards or fails to operate in a manner consistent with state insurance laws. (p. 2.20)

Application Question

9-4. In some states, insurer customer service representatives who respond to customers' questions are required to have insurance agent's licenses. Based on the reasons for insurance licensing, why could this be a benefit for a policyholder of that state? (p. 2.20)

Educational Objective 10
Explain how the excess and surplus lines market meets the needs of various classes of business that are often unable to find insurance in the standard market.

Key Words and Phrases
Standard market (p. 2.21)

Excess and surplus lines (E&S) insurance (p. 2.21)

Nonadmitted insurer, or unlicensed insurer (p. 2.23)

Review Questions

10-1. What types of exposures might be insured in the excess and surplus lines market? (p. 2.22)

10-2. Explain how an excess and surplus lines (E&S) insurer would handle the following exposures: (p. 2.22)

a. An unusual or unique exposure, such as a singer who does not show up for a performance.

b. A nonstandard business loss exposure, such as a restaurant that has a history of grease fires in its kitchen and whose standard insurer has nonrenewed its policy because of poor loss experience.

10-3. What methods are used in many states to regulate the operation of nonadmitted insurers? (p. 2.23)

Application Question

10-4. Atwell Insurance Company, specializing in insuring traveling carnivals, has been operating in Texas for ten years. The executives at Atwell have decided to expand their business to arcades and carnivals nationwide. Why might this insurer elect to enter the excess and surplus lines insurance market? (pp. 2.22–2.23)

Educational Objective 11

Summarize the historical and present-day effect on insurance regulation of the following court decisions, legislation passed, and legislation under review:

a. U.S. Supreme Court decision in the *South-Eastern Underwriters Association* case

b. McCarran-Ferguson Act

c. Gramm-Leach-Bliley Act

d. State Modernization and Regulatory Transparency Act (SMART Act)

Review Questions

11-1. After the Supreme Court decision in the *South-Eastern Underwriters Association* case opened the door to federal regulation of the insurance industry, what action reversed that decision? (Course Guide Reading 2-1)

11-2. Does the Gramm-Leach-Bliley Act contradict the McCarran-Ferguson Act? Why or why not? (Course Guide Reading 2-1)

Application Questions

11-3. Chuck works in the Statistical Reporting and Regulatory Department of the Fernley Insurance Group. He oversees a group that must file insurance reports with fifty different state insurance departments. Chuck says "I hope that the SMART Act becomes reality, so that I can report just to one federal overseer instead of fifty different states with unique requirements." Would passage of SMART fulfill Chuck's wishes? (Course Guide Reading 2-1)

11-4. Henry Kim is considering buying an insurance policy from XYZ Insurance Company. Henry wants to be sure he is paying a fair price for his insurance, and he also wants to be sure his claims will be paid. Explain how, if at all, each of the following facts provides assurances for Henry and other policyholders. (Educational Objectives 3 and 6)

   a. Henry's state has a use-and-file rating law.

b. XYZ Insurance Company is periodically audited by state regulatory authorities.

c. An insurance guaranty fund is in operation in Henry's state.

Answers to Assignment 2 Questions

NOTE: These answers are provided to give students a basic understanding of acceptable types of responses. They often are not the only valid answers and are not intended to provide an exhaustive response to the questions.

Educational Objective 1

1-1. a. A distinctive feature of a stock insurer is that it is formed for the purpose of earning a profit for its stockholders.
   b. A distinctive feature of a mutual insurer is that it provides insurance to its policyholders who are the owners.
   c. A distinctive feature of a reciprocal insurance exchange is that it is managed by an attorney-in-fact.
   d. A distinctive feature of Lloyd's is that it provides facilities for its members to write insurance (a marketplace).
   e. A distinctive feature of American Lloyds is that these associations have limited liability.
   f. A distinctive feature of a captive insurer is that it is formed to provide insurance for its parent company.
   g. A distinctive feature of a reinsurance company is that it accepts the loss exposures transferred by primary insurers for a premium.

1-2. Corporations may use a captive insurer for the following reasons:
   - To lower costs for coverage
   - To ease insurance availability problems
   - To improve cash flow

1-3.
   - An insurer might buy reinsurance to permit the primary insurer to transfer some of its loss exposures with the reinsurer.
   - A small insurer might buy reinsurance to provide insurance for large accounts that would otherwise exceed the insurer's capacity.

Educational Objective 2

2-1. An example of how some federal insurance programs serve the public in a manner that only the government can is their ability to tax in order to provide the financial resources needed to insure some loss exposures. The government also has the power to make the system viable by making participation mandatory.

2-2. The Social Security program is a federal insurance program that provides benefits for eligible citizens (retirement benefits for the elderly, survivorship benefits for dependents of deceased workers, disability payments for disabled workers, and medical benefits for the elderly).

2-3. The Social Security program is a comprehensive program that provides benefits to millions of eligible U.S. citizens. The federal government can make participation mandatory, generating enormous revenues to operate the system.

Educational Objective 3

3-1.
- The Federal Crop Insurance Program is a federal insurance program that covers crop exposures for farmers in areas subject to hailstorms.
- The National Flood Insurance Program is a federal insurance program that covers property in areas exposed to flooding.

3-2. A pharmaceutical company's losses because of a drug's side effects could be catastrophic, creating exposures that private insurers would avoid. In that sense, this resembles a loss exposure the federal government might insure.

Educational Objective 4

4-1.
- Unemployment insurance programs are state insurance programs that provide loss-of-income coverage for eligible workers in the state.
- Automobile insurance plans are state insurance programs that provide coverage for applicants having difficulty obtaining automobile insurance (because of poor driving records or little or no driving experience); they spread the cost among all private insurers writing auto insurance in the state.
- FAIR plans are state insurance plans that provide property insurance where it would otherwise be unavailable; they spread the cost among all private insurers writing property insurance in the state.

4-2. The first type of state workers' compensation insurance fund is the monopolistic state fund, which is the only source of workers' compensation insurance allowed in the state. The second type of state workers' compensation insurance fund is the competitive state fund, in which employers choose between the state fund or some other means of meeting their obligations under workers' compensation statutes. The third type of state workers' compensation insurance fund is the residual market plan, which is a program offered to applicants who are unable to obtain insurance from a private insurer; the applicant applies to the state fund to obtain coverage.

4-3. Guaranty funds provide coverage for the unpaid claims of insolvent insurers licensed in the state. They are funded by assessments against other licensed insurers.

4-4. The loss exposures that these programs cover are unique to various states. The FAIR plans provide access to property insurance in urban areas, which is a problem in only selected states. The beach-front and windstorm pools are needed only in those states with those exposures. Each state is in a unique position to analyze its own exposures and address those exposures.

Educational Objective 5

5-1. The members of the NAIC are the heads (usually called commissioners) of the insurance departments of each of the fifty states and the District of Columbia. (The commissioners of Puerto Rico, Guam, American Samoa, and the U.S. Virgin Islands also belong to the NAIC.)

5-2. The National Association of Insurance Commissioners encourages coordination and cooperation among state insurance departments with the following services:
- Developing model laws, written in a style similar to that of a state statute, that reflect the NAIC's proposed solution to a given problem or issue

- Creating a uniform financial statement for property-casualty insurers
- Implementing an accreditation program to ensure that states have the appropriate legislation and authority to regulate the solvency of the insurance industry

5-3. The three primary objectives of insurance regulation are rate regulation, solvency surveillance, and consumer protection.

5-4. Each state has unique exposures and concerns that must be addressed. By creating model laws there is some level of continuity. By allowing flexibility in their implementation, state legislatures can customize the statutes to meet their unique needs.

Educational Objective 6

6-1. A rate is the price for purchasing insurance coverage for one unit of exposure. A premium is the total amount paid by the insured to the insurer for insurance coverage of an entire exposure for a given period. The premium is the product of the rate times the number of exposure units. For a given rate, the premium will increase as the number of exposure units increases.

6-2. To determine the premiums to charge, insurers predict, as accurately as possible, the expenses they will incur to pay for losses. Insurers also add an amount sufficient to cover the expected administrative costs of company operations to the predicted loss expenses. In addition, the premium includes a charge for profits and contingencies, such as possible catastrophic losses. This amount is generally modified to reflect the investment income that can be earned on the funds held for future claim payments.

6-3. Insurers use rate classification systems to differentiate among insureds based on each insured's loss potential. For example, insureds with frame houses are placed in one classification for fire insurance and insureds with brick houses are placed in another, because the probable severity of a fire loss is greater for a frame house.

6-4. The differences could be attributed to differing loss exposures or hazards associated with the two automobiles. The predicted losses might be greater for one automobile than the other. For example, one automobile might have a driver who has had traffic violations or accidents that indicate the increased probability of a future loss. The rate charged for this automobile would be higher.

Educational Objective 7

7-1. Three objectives of rate regulation are to ensure that rates are as follows:
- Adequate
- Not excessive
- Not unfairly discriminatory

7-2. The goal of rate adequacy conflicts with pressures to hold down insurance premiums because an insurer may have difficulty competing if its rates are substantially higher than those charged by other insurers providing similar coverage and service. Also, although insurance regulators desire rate adequacy to maintain insurer solvency, other pressures encourage regulators to keep rates low.

7-3. Actuaries would calculate higher rates for the loss experience of young male drivers than young female drivers because the young male drivers have worse auto accident records. Actuarial equity concepts would allow insurers to apply higher rates to young male drivers because of their greater loss experience.

Social equity concepts would hold that it is unfairly discriminatory to require a young male driver to pay a higher rate because of his gender and age.

7-4. One of the objectives of rate regulation is to ensure that rates are not unfair.

Educational Objective 8

8-1.
- Prior-approval laws specify that insurers must file proposed rates with the state insurance department to obtain approval to use those rates.
- Flex rating laws specify that prior approval for rates is required only if the new rates are a specified percentage above or below previously filed rates.
- File-and-use laws specify that insurers must file proposed rates with the state insurance department, but they do not need to wait for approval to begin using the rates.
- Use-and-file laws specify that rates must be filed within a specified period of time after they are first used in the state.
- Open competition (no-file laws) specify that rates do not have to be filed with the state.
- A state-mandated rate is a system that requires all insurers to use rates established by the state insurance department for a particular type of insurance.

8-2.
- Exempt commercial policyholders are organizations of sufficient size and sophistication that they can buy some types of insurance using rates and/or forms not filed with state regulators.
- Non-filed inland marine classes are exempt from filing requirements because the types of exposures can vary greatly from one insured to the next, such that using standard forms and rates is impractical.
- Excess and surplus lines insurance coverage is provided by insurers that are exempt from rate and form regulation, when needed insurance is not available in the standard market.

Educational Objective 9

9-1. Insurance regulators monitor the solvency of insurers doing business in their states by the following methods:
- Using insurer examinations that analyze an insurer's operations and financial condition
- Using the Insurance Regulatory Information System (IRIS), which helps regulators identify insurers with potential financial problems

9-2. State regulators protect insurance consumers by the following activities:
   a. Licensing insurers and revoking or suspending an insurer's license if an insurer fails to meet financial standards or fails to operate in a manner consistent with state insurance laws
   b. Licensing insurer representatives to ensure they have a prescribed minimum level of insurance knowledge
   c. Approving policy forms that prevent insurers from including unfair or unreasonable provisions in insurance policies

> d. Examining market conduct to identify insurers having unfair underwriting or claim practices and by fining, suspending, or revoking the operating licenses of insurers guilty of these abuses
> e. Investigating consumer complaints, holding formal hearings to determine whether the complaints are valid, and taking appropriate action

9-3. If an insurer fails to meet financial standards or fails to operate in a manner consistent with state insurance laws, state regulators have the authority to revoke or suspend the company's license to protect consumers' interests.

9-4. Licensing and continuing education ensures a level of knowledge of insurance professionals who complete the requirements. Policyholders of that state would benefit from receiving information from customer service representatives who have attained at least that base level of knowledge.

Educational Objective 10

10-1. The excess and surplus lines market might insure the following types of exposures:
- Unusual or unique loss exposures
- Nonstandard business
- Insureds needing high limits
- Insureds needing unusually broad coverage
- Loss exposures that require new forms

10-2. a. An excess and surplus lines (E&S) insurer could write coverage for an unusual or unique exposure, such as for a singer who does not show up for a performance. This "nonappearance insurance" covers the losses of the production or show sponsors if the performer named in the policy fails to appear because of a covered cause, such as injury, illness, or death.
b. An E&S insurer facing a nonstandard business loss exposure, such as a restaurant that has a history of grease fires in its kitchen and whose standard insurer has nonrenewed its policy because of poor loss experience, may be willing to write insurance for this restaurant with a premium substantially higher than a standard insurer would charge.

10-3. Some states maintain lists of E&S insurers that are approved (or not approved) to do business in the state. Most states have surplus lines laws requiring all E&S business to be placed through an E&S broker. The E&S broker is licensed by the state to transact business through nonadmitted insurers.

10-4. If the insurer decided to become licensed in each state, its rates and policy forms would have to be approved in each state. By being nonadmitted, Atwell has more flexibility to provide the coverage forms and the rates that the market requires. Atwell may also be able to market through an E&S broker more effectively than attempting to market its policies independently.

Educational Objective 11

11-1. The passage by Congress of the McCarran-Ferguson Act effectively reversed the decision from the Supreme Court in the *South-Eastern Underwriters Association* case. McCarran-Ferguson provides that insurers are generally exempt from federal antitrust laws, leaving the regulation of insurers to the individual states.

11-2. The Gramm-Leach-Bliley Act does not contradict the McCarran-Ferguson Act. While it does promote uniform producer licensing laws, it also reaffirms the McCarran-Ferguson Act. GLB attempts to reconcile federal banking and security laws with a state regulatory system for the insurance industry.

11-3. Chuck is likely to be partly satisfied if the SMART Act becomes law. He will still need to make reports to fifty states, but SMART could mandate uniform provisions that would make it much easier because fulfilling regulatory requirements should be similar from state to state.

11-4. a. Henry and other policyholders can be assured that they are paying a fair price for their insurance because Henry's state has a use-and-file rating law; therefore, state regulators are monitoring XYZ's insurance rates and may require changes if a rate change is considered inappropriate.

b. Henry and other policyholders can be assured that their claims will be paid because XYZ is periodically audited by state regulators who are monitoring XYZ's financial condition and will take steps if they see danger signs.

c. Henry and other policyholders can be assured that their claims will be paid because Henry's state has an insurance guaranty fund in operation; therefore, they should be able to have their claims paid by the guaranty fund if XYZ becomes insolvent.

Direct Your Learning

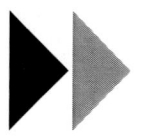

Assignment 3

Measuring the Financial Performance of Insurers

Educational Objectives

After learning the content of this assignment, you should be able to:

1. Describe the sources of income for a property-casualty insurer.
2. Describe the types of expenses that a property-casualty insurer incurs.
3. Explain how an insurer's gain or loss from operations is determined.
4. Distinguish between the admitted and nonadmitted assets of insurers.
5. Describe the three types of liabilities found on the financial statements of insurers.
6. Describe the typical items found on the balance sheet of a property-casualty insurer.
7. Describe the typical items found on the income statement of a property-casualty insurer.
8. Given an insurer's financial statements, calculate and explain the significance of the following profitability ratios:
   a. Loss ratio
   b. Expense ratio
   c. Dividend ratio
   d. Combined ratio
   e. Investment income ratio
   f. Overall operating ratio
9. Given an insurer's financial statements, calculate and explain the significance of an insurer's capacity ratio.
10. Define or describe each of the Key Words and Phrases for this assignment.

Study Materials

Required Reading:
- Property and Liability Insurance Principles
  - Chapter 3

Study Aids:
- SMART Online Practice Exams
- SMART Study Aids
  - Review Notes and Flash Cards—Assignment 3

Outline

▶ **Insurer Profitability**
   A. Underwriting Income
   B. Investment Income
   C. Expenses
      1. Losses
      2. Loss Adjustment Expenses
      3. Other Underwriting Expenses
      4. Dividends
      5. Investment Expenses
   D. Gain or Loss From Operations
      1. Net Income Before Taxes
      2. Income Taxes
      3. Net Income or Loss

▶ **Insurer Solvency**
   A. Assets
      1. Admitted Assets
      2. Nonadmitted Assets
   B. Liabilities
      1. Loss Reserve and Loss Expense Reserve
      2. Unearned Premium Reserve
      3. Other Liabilities
   C. Policyholders' Surplus

▶ **Monitoring Insurer Financial Performance**
   A. Financial Statements
      1. Balance Sheet
      2. Income Statement
   B. Financial Statement Analysis
      1. Profitability Ratios
      2. Capacity Ratio

▶ **Summary**

s.m.a.r.t. tips

Actively capture information by using the open space in the SMART Review Notes to write out key concepts. Putting information into your own words is an effective way to push that information into your memory.

For each assignment, you should define or describe each of the Key Words and Phrases and answer each of the Review and Application Questions.

Educational Objective 1
Describe the sources of income for a property-casualty insurer.

Review Questions

1-1. What are an insurer's two major income sources? (p. 3.3)

1-2. What is the distinction between written premiums and earned premiums? (p. 3.4)

1-3. What funds provide an insurer's two major sources of investment income? (p. 3.5)

3.4 Property and Liability Insurance Principles—INS 21

Application Questions

1-4. Assume that you are the executive for an insurer attempting to measure the success of a promotional program to sell insurance to large businesses. Explain whether you would use written premiums or earned premiums to measure the amount of insurance sold, and therefore the program's success. (p. 3.4)

1-5. On April 1, the XYZ Insurance Company issued a policy with a one-year policy period. The premium for the policy was $6,000. On December 31 of the same year, what was the amount of each of the following for this policy? (p. 3.4)

   a. Written premiums

   b. Earned premiums

   c. Unearned premiums

Measuring the Financial Performance of Insurers 3.5

Educational Objective 2
Describe the types of expenses that a property-casualty insurer incurs.

Key Words and Phrases

Paid loss (p. 3.7)

Incurred losses (p. 3.7)

Loss reserves (p. 3.7)

Review Questions

2-1. What types of expenses does an insurer incur? (pp. 3.6–3.9)

2-2. Of the following insurer expenses for a specific policy, which are incurred at the beginning of the policy term, and which may occur throughout the policy term? Explain. (pp. 3.7–3.8)

   a. Acquisition expenses

   b. Loss expenses

Educational Objective 3

Explain how an insurer's gain or loss from operations is determined.

Key Words and Phrases

Net investment gain or loss (p. 3.9)

Net underwriting gain or loss (p. 3.9)

Overall gain or loss from operations (p. 3.9)

Review Question

3-1. Would you agree that net underwriting gain or loss provides the best measure of an insurer's performance in conducting the business of insurance even though the overall gain or loss from operations gives a better measure of its overall financial performance? Explain why or why not. (pp. 3.9–3.10)

Application Question

3-2. Spring Insurance Company writes property insurance in a state with a history of tornadoes. After a particularly active tornado season, several other property insurers withdrew from the state because of the losses that they had sustained. In a six-month period following the storm season, Spring received four times the number of property applications that it normally receives. Spring's executives were concerned that the company was growing too fast. Considering the expenses that an insurer incurs, explain why the executives might have made such a statement. (pp. 3.6–3.9)

Educational Objective 4

Distinguish between the admitted and nonadmitted assets of insurers.

Key Words and Phrases

Assets (p. 3.11)

Admitted assets (p. 3.11)

Nonadmitted assets (p. 3.11)

Review Questions

4-1. Why are nonadmitted assets not counted as assets on the financial statements required by insurance regulators? (p. 3.11)

4-2. Provide three examples of admitted assets and three examples of nonadmitted assets. (p. 3.11)

4-3. What do the creation of the two categories of assets, admitted and nonadmitted, reflect? (p. 3.11)

Application Question

4-4. XYZ Insurance constructed a new office building and moved its operations into the building. XYZ's executives were disappointed to learn that the brand-new furniture they purchased for the new location was a nonadmitted asset. The cash that XYZ invested in the furniture moved from being an admitted asset to a nonadmitted asset; therefore, XYZ's overall admitted assets declined. Explain whether the change in XYZ's balance sheet was fair. (p. 3.11)

Educational Objective 5

Describe the three types of liabilities found on the financial statements of insurers.

Key Words and Phrases

Liabilities (p. 3.11)

Loss reserve (p. 3.12)

Unearned premium reserve (p. 3.12)

Policyholders' surplus (p. 3.12)

Review Questions

5-1. Reserves are money being held by the insurer. Why are loss reserves and unearned premium reserves listed on the balance sheet as liabilities rather than as assets? (p. 3.12)

5-2. Despite its name, an insurer's policyholders' surplus is not leftover money. Why is policyholders' surplus an important measure of the insurer's financial well-being? (p. 3.12)

5-3. Describe two purposes that policyholders' surplus serves. (p. 3.12)

Application Question

5-4. After Fernley Insurance Company launched a marketing campaign for personal automobile insurance, the company tripled its number of policies written in one year. During this period of growth, if the ratio of losses remained constant, explain whether Fernley's policyholders' surplus is likely to increase or decrease. (p. 3.12)

Educational Objective 6
Describe the typical items found on the balance sheet of a property-casualty insurer.

Key Word or Phrase
Balance sheet (p. 3.14)

Review Questions

6-1. Describe the time period represented by an insurer's balance sheet. (p. 3.14)

6-2. What items are typically found on an insurer's balance sheet? (p. 3.14)

6-3. Provide two examples of how an insurer's assets and liabilities can change on a balance sheet. (p. 3.14)

6-4. Describe how an insurer meets its financial obligations while earning investment income. (p. 3.14)

Application Question

6-5. Josue is an underwriter with the XYZ Insurance Company. Josue is looking for information about the total value of XYZ's assets at the end of the last calendar year. Explain whether XYZ's balance sheet would provide that information to Josue. (p. 3.14)

Educational Objective 7

Describe the typical items found on the income statement of a property-casualty insurer.

Key Word or Phrase

Income statement (p. 3.15)

Review Questions

7-1. What items are typically found on an insurer's income statement? (p. 3.15)

7-2. Describe a situation in which an insurer would incur a net underwriting loss. (p. 3.15)

Application Question

7-3. Harold is reviewing the financial strength of several insurers to determine where he would like to insure his large commercial account. He has determined that most of the companies have had net underwriting losses for the past three years, which concerns Harold. Explain why Harold should also review the income statements for these insurers to gain a more complete view of their net income. (p. 3.15)

Educational Objective 8

Given an insurer's financial statements, calculate and explain the significance of the following profitability ratios:

a. Loss ratio
b. Expense ratio
c. Dividend ratio
d. Combined ratio
e. Investment income ratio
f. Overall operating ratio

Key Words and Phrases

Loss ratio (p. 3.16)

Expense ratio (p. 3.16)

Dividend ratio (p. 3.17)

Combined ratio (p. 3.17)

Investment income ratio (p. 3.18)

Overall operating ratio (p. 3.18)

Review Questions

8-1. Explain how the following entities use ratios to highlight a particular aspect of financial performance. (pp. 3.15–3.16)

   a. Insurer managers

   b. Investors

   c. Regulators

8-2. Explain what each of the following ratios indicates about an insurer's performance and show the mathematical formula that is used to compute that ratio. (pp. 3.16–3.20)

   a. Loss ratio

   b. Expense ratio

c. Dividend ratio

d. Combined ratio

e. Investment income ratio

f. Overall operating ratio

Application Questions

8-3. The following information has been compiled on the basis of the income statement and balance sheet of the XYZ Insurance Company: (pp. 3.16–3.18)

Earned premiums	$ 9,000,000
Written premiums	$10,000,000
Incurred expenses	$ 3,000,000
Incurred losses	$ 7,200,000

Calculate the following ratios for XYZ Insurance Company:

a. Expense ratio

b. Loss ratio

c. Combined ratio

8-4. XYZ Insurance Company has an overall operating ratio of 95 percent. What does that ratio indicate about XYZ Insurance Company's profitability? (pp. 3.18–3.19)

Educational Objective 9

Given an insurer's financial statements, calculate and explain the significance of an insurer's capacity ratio.

Key Word or Phrase

Capacity ratio, or premium-to-surplus ratio (p. 3.20)

Review Questions

9-1. Show the calculation for an insurer's capacity ratio. (p. 3.20)

9-2. Regarding the capacity ratio, what do the following items represent? (p. 3.20)

   a. Written premiums

   b. Policyholders' surplus

9-3. Explain what an insurer must do if losses and expenses exceed written premiums. (p. 3.20)

9-4. How do insurance regulators use the capacity ratio? (p. 3.20)

Application Question

9-5. The following information has been compiled regarding XYZ Insurance Company's income statement and balance sheet: (p. 3.20)

Earned premiums:	$250,000,000
Written premiums:	$300,000,000
Policyholders' surplus:	$100,000,000

a. Calculate XYZ's capacity ratio.

b. Explain what this capacity ratio tells you about XYZ.

Answers to Assignment 3 Questions

NOTE: These answers are provided to give students a basic understanding of acceptable types of responses. They often are not the only valid answers and are not intended to provide an exhaustive response to the questions.

Educational Objective 1

1-1. An insurer's two major income sources include the following:
- Underwriting income from the sale of insurance
- Investment income

1-2. Written premiums are the total amount of premiums for policies put into effect during a given period. Earned premiums for a specific policy are the part of the written premiums that apply to the part of the policy period that has already occurred.

1-3. Two major sources of an insurer's investment income include the following funds:
- Policyholders' surplus
- Premiums not used yet to pay claims

1-4. You would probably use earned premiums, which reflect the ultimate result. If the new program resulted in many cancellations, the earned premiums would be much lower than the written premiums and a more complete picture of the program's success.

1-5.   a. The written premiums were $6,000, the amount the insured was billed at the beginning of the policy period.

   b. The earned premiums were approximately $4,500, because nine of the twelve months of coverage had elapsed.

   $$\frac{9}{12} = \frac{3}{4} = 0.75$$

   $0.75 \times \$6,000 = \$4,500.$

   c. The unearned premiums were approximately $1,500, because three months of coverage remained.

   $$\frac{3}{12} = \frac{1}{4} = 0.25$$

   $0.25 \times \$6,000 = \$1,500.$

Educational Objective 2

2-1. An insurer incurs the following types of expenses:
- Losses (including expenses for investigating and settling claims)
- Other underwriting expenses (acquisition expenses, general expenses, premium taxes, licenses, and fees)
- Investment expenses

2-2. a. An acquisition expense is an insurer expense that is incurred at the beginning of the policy term (for example, sales commissions and advertising expenses).

b. A loss expense is an insurer expense that occurs throughout the policy term (for example, claim costs to repair or replace property, medical expenses, investigation costs, legal fees, and adjuster fees).

Educational Objective 3

3-1. Agree. The overall gain or loss from operations is affected by investment gains or losses that have nothing to do with how well the insurer conducts its marketing, underwriting, or claims activities.

3-2. Acquisition expenses are significant for an insurer. Spring must pay the cost of processing the policies as well as commissions to the agents or producers who submitted the policies. In addition, the premiums on these new policies must be earned. While the premiums are unearned initially, Spring may be paying more in acquisition expenses than it is earning in premiums.

Educational Objective 4

4-1. Nonadmitted assets are not counted as assets on the financial statements required by insurance regulators because, if the insurer were to liquidate its holdings, the nonadmitted assets could not readily be converted to cash at or near their market value.

4-2. Three examples of admitted assets include stocks, bonds, and mortgages. Others include certain computer equipment and premium balances due in less than ninety days. Three examples of nonadmitted assets include office equipment, furniture and supplies, and premiums that are more than ninety days overdue.

4-3. The creation of the two categories of assets, admitted and nonadmitted, reflects the financially conservative view that insurance regulators take when evaluating an insurer's financial strength.

4-4. XYZ cannot easily liquidate the furniture assets. Therefore, the change in the balance sheet was accurate, it was in accord with the principles of statutory accounting, and it presents a clear picture of XYZ's finances.

Educational Objective 5

5-1. Both loss reserves and unearned premium reserves are listed on the balance sheet as liabilities because they represent financial obligations (liabilities) owed by the insurer. The loss reserve estimates the final settlement amount on all claims that have occurred but have not yet been settled. The unearned premium reserve represents insurance premiums paid by insureds for services that the insurer has not yet rendered.

5-2. Policyholders' surplus is an important measure of the insurer's financial well-being because it is the difference between what the insurer owns and what it owes.

5-3. Policyholders' surplus serves two purposes. First, it provides a cushion that is available in case the insurer has adverse financial experience. Second, it provides the necessary resources if the insurer decides to expand into a new territory or develop new insurance products.

5-4. Fernley's policyholders' surplus is likely to decrease. Its policyholders' surplus equals its admitted assets minus its total liabilities. One of the liabilities is the unearned premium reserve. Because so many new policies are being written, Fernley will have a large unearned premium reserve that nearly offsets the premiums collected on the new policies. In addition, Fernley will have significant acquisition expenses that will reduce its assets and policyholders' surplus.

Educational Objective 6

6-1. The balance sheet is a financial statement that shows an insurer's financial position at a particular time.

6-2. The following items are typically found on an insurer's balance sheet:
- Admitted assets
- Liabilities
- Policyholders' surplus

6-3. One example in which an insurer's assets and liabilities can change on a balance sheet is insurers establishing unearned premium reserves for premiums they receive. The unearned premium reserve for each policy decreases over time. Another example is when a loss occurs and an insurer establishes loss reserves.

6-4. An insurer meets its financial obligations while earning investment income by buying and selling stocks, bonds, and other investments as needed.

6-5. The balance sheet shows a company's financial position at a particular time. Josue will find the information he seeks only on the balance sheet that was completed on December 31 of that year.

Educational Objective 7

7-1. The following items are typically found on an insurer's income statement:
- Revenues (earned premiums and investment income)
- Expenses
- Net income

7-2. An insurer would incur a net underwriting loss if losses and underwriting expenses exceeded earned premiums.

7-3. The net underwriting gain or loss is calculated using only earned premiums minus total expenses. Income statements include earned premiums, expenses, and net investment income. With the inclusion of the net investment income, companies with underwriting losses may be generating a net operating gain.

Educational Objective 8

8-1. a. Insurer managers use ratios to identify strengths and weaknesses in their companies' operations.
   b. Investors use ratios to identify the insurers that are most attractive as investments.
   c. Regulators use ratios to determine whether insurers have the financial strength to remain viable in the long term and to meet their financial obligations to policyholders and other parties.

8-2. a. The loss ratio compares an insurer's incurred losses to its earned premiums for a specific time period. The figure for incurred losses includes loss adjustment expenses. The loss ratio is defined as follows:

$$\text{Loss ratio} = \frac{\text{Incurred losses (including loss adjustment expenses)}}{\text{Earned premiums}}.$$

b. The expense ratio is a profitability ratio that shows the insurer's cost of doing business as a proportion of written premiums.

$$\text{Expense ratio} = \frac{\text{Incurred underwriting expenses}}{\text{Written premiums}}.$$

c. The dividend ratio indicates what proportion of an insurer's earned premiums (if any) is being returned to policyholders in the form of dividends.

$$\text{Dividend ratio} = \frac{\text{Policyholder dividends}}{\text{Earned premiums}}.$$

d. The combined ratio is a profitability ratio that indicates the insurer's underwriting performance.

Combined ratio = Loss ratio + Expense ratio

$$= \frac{\text{Incurred losses (including loss adjustment expenses)}}{\text{Earned premiums}} + \frac{\text{Incurred underwriting expenses}}{\text{Written premiums}}.$$

For insurers that pay policyholder dividends (not stock dividends), the third component of the combined ratio is the dividend ratio. Hence, the formula is:

Combined ratio = Loss ratio + Expense ratio + Dividend ratio.

e. The investment income ratio is a profitability ratio that indicates the insurer's degree of success achieved in investment activities.

$$\text{Investment income ratio} = \frac{\text{Net investment income}}{\text{Earned premiums}}.$$

f. The overall operating ratio indicates the insurer's profitability.

Overall operating ratio = Combined ratio − Investment income ratio

$$= \frac{\text{Incurred losses (including loss adjustment expenses)}}{\text{Earned premiums}} + \frac{\text{Incurred underwriting expenses}}{\text{Written premiums}} - \frac{\text{Net investment income}}{\text{Earned premiums}}.$$

8-3. a. Expense ratio = $\dfrac{\text{Incurred expenses}}{\text{Written premiums}} = \dfrac{\$3,000,000}{\$10,000,000} = 0.3$ (or 30%).

b. Loss ratio = $\dfrac{\text{Incurred losses}}{\text{Earned premiums}} = \dfrac{\$7,200,000}{\$9,000,000} = 0.8$ (or 80%).

c. Combined ratio = Expense ratio + Loss ratio = 0.30 + 0.80 = 1.10 (or 110%).

8-4. XYZ Insurance Company's overall operating ratio of 95 percent indicates an overall operating gain with revenues greater than total expenses.

Educational Objective 9

9-1. An insurer's capacity ratio is calculated as follows:

$$\text{Capacity ratio} = \dfrac{\text{Written premiums}}{\text{Policyholders' surplus}}.$$

9-2. a. Regarding capacity ratios, written premiums represent the insurer's exposure to potential claims.

b. In relation to capacity ratios, policyholders' surplus represents the insurer's cushion for absorbing adverse results.

9-3. If losses and expenses exceed written premiums, an insurer must use its surplus to meet its obligations. Therefore, an insurer's new written premiums should not become too large relative to its policyholders' surplus.

9-4. Insurance regulators use the capacity ratio as a benchmark to determine whether an insurer might be headed toward financial difficulty.

9-5. a. Capacity ratio = $\dfrac{\text{Written premiums}}{\text{Policyholders' surplus}} = \dfrac{\$300,000,000}{\$100,000,000} = \dfrac{3}{1}$.

b. XYZ has a 3-to-1 written premiums to policyholders' surplus ratio. The larger the ratio, the less the capacity XYZ has to write new business. XYZ might be headed for financial difficulty.

SEGMENT B

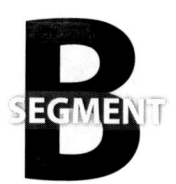

Assignment 4   Marketing

Assignment 5   Underwriting

Assignment 6   Claims

Segment B is the second of three segments in the INS 21 course. These segments are designed to help structure your study.

Direct Your Learning

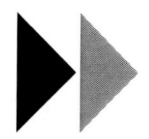

Marketing

Educational Objectives

After learning the content of this assignment, you should be able to:

1. Describe the legal relationship known as agency.

2. Describe the responsibilities of the agent and the principal in any agency relationship.

3. Describe each of the following types of insurance agents' authority:

   a. Express authority

   b. Implied authority

   c. Apparent authority

4. Summarize the various types of insurance marketing systems and alternative distribution channels.

5. Describe typical compensation arrangements for insurance producers.

6. Describe advertising methods used by insurers, producers, and producer trade associations.

7. Describe the various aspects of marketing management.

8. Describe how states regulate producers' activities.

9. Discuss unfair trade practices as they relate to insurance.

10. Define or describe each of the Key Words and Phrases for this assignment.

Study Materials

Required Reading:
- Property and Liability Insurance Principles
  - Chapter 4

Study Aids:
- SMART Online Practice Exams
- SMART Study Aids
  - Review Notes and Flash Cards—Assignment 4

Outline

▶ **The Legal Role of the Insurance Agent**
  A. Creation of the Agency Relationship
  B. Responsibilities of the Agent to the Principal
  C. Responsibilities of the Principal to the Agent
  D. Responsibilities of the Agent and the Principal to Third Parties
  E. Authority of Agents
    1. Express Authority
    2. Implied Authority
    3. Apparent Authority

▶ **Insurance Marketing Systems**
  A. Independent Agency System
    1. Independent Agents
    2. Independent Agencies That Represent Only One Insurer
    3. Brokers
    4. Managing General Agencies (MGAs)
  B. Exclusive Agency System
  C. Direct Writing System
  D. Alternative Distribution Channels
    1. Direct Response
    2. Internet
    3. Call Centers
    4. Group Marketing
    5. Financial Institutions
  E. Mixed Marketing System

▶ **Producer Compensation**
  A. Sales Commissions
  B. Contingent Commissions

▶ **Advertising**
  A. Producers' Trade Associations
    1. Independent Agents' Trade Associations
    2. Agents' and Brokers' Trade Association
    3. Managing General Agents' Association

▶ **Marketing Management**
  A. Producer Supervision
  B. Producer Motivation
  C. Product Management and Development

▶ **Producer Regulation**
  A. Licensing Laws
  B. Unfair Trade Practices Laws
    1. Misrepresentation and False Advertising
    2. Tie-In Sales
    3. Rebating
    4. Other Deceptive Practices

▶ **Summary**

Use the SMART Online Practice Exams to test your understanding of the course material. You can review questions over a single assignment or multiple assignments, or you can take an exam over the entire course.

Marketing 4.3

For each assignment, you should define or describe each of the Key Words and Phrases and answer each of the Review and Application Questions.

Educational Objective 1
Describe the legal relationship known as agency.

Key Words and Phrases

Producer (p. 4.3)

Agency (p. 4.3)

Agent (p. 4.3)

Principal (p. 4.3)

Insurance agent (p. 4.4)

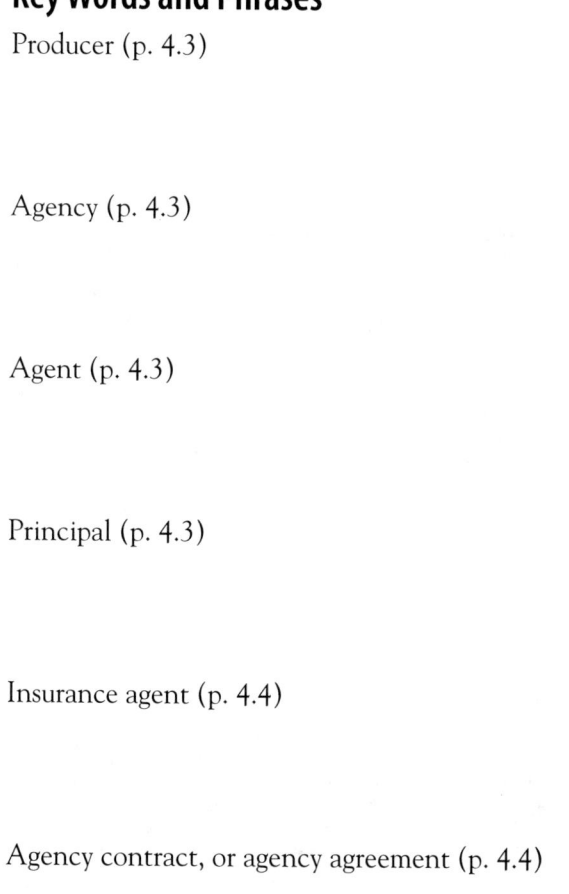

Agency contract, or agency agreement (p. 4.4)

Review Questions

1-1. Describe the two essential elements of an agency relationship. (p. 4.3)

4.4 Property and Liability Insurance Principles—INS 21

1-2. Illustrate the meaning of the following statement: "The principal can authorize the agent to do anything the principal can do." (p. 4.3)

1-3. How is an agency relationship created between an insurer and its agents? (p. 4.4)

Application Question

1-4. Alex owns and manages the Independent Insurance Agency. Alex would like to begin offering payment plans to his customers who have large insurance premiums. Alex has made arrangements with a local bank that will finance the premiums for his customers. How can Alex determine whether this type of arrangement is acceptable to the insurers that he represents? (pp. 4.4–4.5)

Marketing 4.5

Educational Objective 2
Describe the responsibilities of the agent and the principal in any agency relationship.

Key Word or Phrase
Errors and omissions (E&O) (p. 4.5)

Review Questions

2-1. What responsibilities does an insurance agent have towards its principal, the insurer? (pp. 4.4–4.5)

2-2. What responsibilities does an insurer have to its agents? (p. 4.5)

2-3. Insureds are required to notify the insurer as soon as possible when a loss occurs. If an insurance agent is told about a loss but fails to report it to the insurer he or she represents, can the insurer deny its responsibility to pay the claim? Explain. (p. 4.5)

Application Question

2-4. Ruth owns and manages an insurance agency. While she was on vacation, she hired a temporary employee, Kathie, to answer telephone calls and questions. Kathie is not an insurance agent and has no insurance experience. During the week, Kathie misunderstood the extent of her responsibilities and agreed to bind coverage for several policyholders who represented loss exposures not written by the companies the insurance agency represents. Considering the responsibilities of an agent to a principal, explain whether Ruth has violated any of these responsibilities. (pp. 4.4–4.5)

Educational Objective 3

Describe each of the following types of insurance agents' authority:

a. Express authority

b. Implied authority

c. Apparent authority

Key Words and Phrases

Express authority (p. 4.6)

Binding authority (p. 4.6)

Binder (p. 4.6)

Implied authority (p. 4.7)

Apparent authority (p. 4.7)

Review Questions

3-1. Give at least one example of an insurance agent's authority in each of the following categories: (pp. 4.6–4.7)

  a. Express authority

  b. Implied authority

  c. Apparent authority

3-2. Tom called his old friend Carol, a licensed agent of XYZ Insurer, and asked her to insure the car he had just purchased. Tom told Carol he would come to her office the next day to sign an application and pay the premium, but he needed immediate coverage so he could drive the car home. How could Carol meet Tom's need? (p. 4.6)

Application Questions

3-3. Andy, an insurance agent, is authorized by Radley Insurance Company to issue insurance policies providing not more than $100,000 in coverage. Andy issues a Radley Insurance Company policy providing $200,000 in coverage. (p. 4.7)

   a. If there is a claim on the $200,000 policy, would Radley be obligated to pay it? Explain.

   b. What might Radley Insurance do to recover the cost of the claim, if obligated to pay it?

3-4. Don applied for insurance coverage on the contents of his apartment. Don's insurance agent told him, "Coverage is bound and the policy will be mailed to you in a month or so." Don's father later told him he should have gotten coverage immediately, rather than going without an insurance policy for a month. Does Don have coverage for his property? Explain. (pp. 4.6–4.7)

Educational Objective 4
Summarize the various types of insurance marketing systems and alternative distribution channels.

Key Words and Phrases

Independent agency (p. 4.8)

Independent agent (p. 4.9)

Agency expiration list (p. 4.9)

Insurance broker (p. 4.10)

Managing general agency (MGA) (p. 4.10)

Exclusive agent (p. 4.11)

Direct writing system (p. 4.11)

Direct response (p. 4.12)

Mixed marketing system (p. 4.13)

Review Questions

4-1. What are the four traditional marketing systems used by most insurers? (pp. 4.7–4.8)

4-2. Why is an insurance agency's expiration list considered a valuable asset? (p. 4.9)

4-3. What is the major difference between an exclusive agent and a producer in the direct writing system? (pp. 4.9–4.12)

4-4. How can an exclusive agent manage to provide a particular customer with an unusual type of insurance that is not available from the insurer that the exclusive agent represents? (p. 4.11)

4-5. Acquisition expenses were discussed in Assignment 3. What acquisition expenses are avoided by an insurer that markets using the direct response system? (pp. 4.12–4.13)

4-6. Insurer XYZ markets auto insurance to high-risk drivers through independent insurance agents. It also offers insurance directly to insurance buyers through the Internet. What term describes Insurer XYZ's marketing system? (pp. 4.13–4.14)

Application Question

4-7. Ron buys his insurance from a direct writing insurer's sales representative, while Anita deals with an independent agent. Norma, on the other hand, buys her insurance through the mail. Explain whether you agree or disagree with the following reasons for their choices. (pp. 4.7–4.14)

   a. Ron: "Because my sales representative is an employee of the insurer, anything she says literally makes a commitment for the insurer. An independent agent is just an intermediary. An independent agent does not have the authority to make any promises, and the insurer is not required to honor any of the agent's commitments."

   b. Anita: "An independent agent represents many different insurers and offers me a broader selection to choose from, and that helps me get the best deal. Sometimes my agent even changes my policy to a different insurer."

c. Norma: "I figure mail order is the best deal. Because it cuts out the middleman, direct response insurance should have the lowest prices. Besides, an agent does not provide any services that I cannot handle over the telephone with my customer service representative."

Educational Objective 5

Describe typical compensation arrangements for insurance producers.

Key Words and Phrases

Sales commission, or commission (p. 4.14)

Contingent commission (p. 4.15)

Review Questions

5-1. Using the following examples of premium collection, explain how insurance agents collect sales commissions. (pp. 4.14–4.15)

a. The insurer handles billing and collections (direct billing).

b. The agency collects the premiums (agency billing or producer billing).

5-2. What must an insurance agency do to receive the following types of commissions? (pp. 4.14–4.15)

   a. Sales commissions

   b. Contingent commissions

5-3. The commission compensates an agency for not only making the sale but also for providing service before and after the sale. (pp. 4.14–4.15)

   a. Identify services an agency provides before the insurance sale.

   b. Identify services an agency provides after the insurance sale.

Application Question

5-4. The XYZ Insurer offers a preferred homeowners policy that has been exceptionally profitable. XYZ executives have determined that they would like to encourage their independent agents to write more of these policies. However, the executives are also cautious about ensuring that they continue to receive applications from policyholders that are carefully selected and will continue to be profitable. Explain how the XYZ executives can structure an incentive for their independent agents to achieve their goals. (p. 4.15)

Educational Objective 6
Describe advertising methods used by insurers, producers, and producer trade associations.

Review Questions

6-1. Identify the advertising goals of the following entities: (pp. 4.15–4.16)

a. Independent agencies

b. Insurers marketing through the independent agency system

6-2. Describe the advertising strategy used by producers' trade associations. (pp. 4.16–4.17)

6-3. What advertising methods are used by the insurer or agency you know best? (pp. 4.15–4.17)

Application Question

6-4. As the XYZ Insurance Company attempts to promote its preferred homeowners policy, it has launched an advertising campaign using billboards and television spots. However, XYZ uses an independent agency system to market its policies. Explain how the XYZ advertising campaign can promote policy sales, even though the policies are sold by independent agents. (p. 4.16)

Educational Objective 7

Describe the various aspects of marketing management.

Key Words and Phrases

Marketing representative (p. 4.17)

Production underwriter (p. 4.17)

Review Questions

7-1. How do insurers supervise their producers? (p. 4.17)

7-2. What do insurers do to encourage insurance agents to sell their products? (p. 4.18)

7-3. Explain how a home office marketing department determines what insurance coverage, price, and services to provide. (p. 4.18)

Application Question

7-4. The XYZ Insurance Company has experienced poor sales results for its policies designed for small business owners. They have been unable to determine why the product is not successfully competing against similar products offered by other insurers. Explain how XYZ can involve its producers in identifying and correcting the problems with this product line. (p. 4.18)

Educational Objective 8
Describe how states regulate producers' activities.

Review Questions

8-1. Explain how state insurance departments regulate insurance producers' activities. (pp. 4.18–4.19)

8-2. What must insurance producers generally do to obtain a license to sell insurance? (p. 4.19)

8-3. What must insurance producers generally do to retain a license to sell insurance? (pp. 4.19)

Application Question

8-4. Consider the following statement: "Examination qualifications to become a licensed insurance agent are unnecessary. Agents can learn processes and procedures as they perform the job as an agent." Explain whether a change to eliminate insurance agent examinations would serve the public interest. (p. 4.19)

Educational Objective 9
Discuss unfair trade practices as they relate to insurance.

Key Words and Phrases
Unfair trade practices law (p. 4.19)

Rebating (p. 4.20)

Review Questions

9-1. What specific unfair trade practices are prohibited for insurance producers? (pp. 4.19–4.21)

9-2. Briefly describe the unfair trade practices law concerning misrepresentation and false advertising for insurance agents or other insurance personnel. (p. 4.20)

9-3. Patty purchased a car from Dean, a salesperson with a car dealership. Dean also holds an insurance agent's license with XYZ Insurance Company (XYZ). Dean tried to coerce Patty to purchase insurance from XYZ by telling Patty that the loan on her new car would be denied unless Patty purchased a policy from XYZ. Explain the unfair trade practices law that prohibits this behavior. (p. 4.20)

9-4. Identify two behaviors that fall under the "other deceptive practices" category of the unfair trade practices laws. (p. 4.21)

Application Question

9-5. Some insurance policies cover a wide range of perils. All perils, or risks, are covered except those that are specifically excluded. The term "all-risks" insurance, which was once used to describe these policies, is being replaced by other terms, such as "special coverage" or "special perils." Explain how the term "all-risks" may have been a violation of unfair trade practices laws.
(pp. 4.20–4.21)

Answers to Assignment 4 Questions

NOTE: These answers are provided to give students a basic understanding of acceptable types of responses. They often are not the only valid answers and are not intended to provide an exhaustive response to the questions.

Educational Objective 1

1-1. Authority and control are the two essential elements of an agency relationship. While the agent has authority to act for the principal, the principal has control over the agent's actions on the principal's behalf.

1-2. The statement "The principal can authorize the agent to do anything the principal can do" is illustrated by an insurer (the principal) that authorizes its agent to collect premiums from insureds for new insurance policies and then requires the agent to remit those premiums (sometimes after deducting a commission) to the insurer within a certain amount of time.

1-3. An agency is created with an agency contract between the agency and the insurer. The agency contract gives the agent the right to represent the insurer and sell insurance on the insurer's behalf.

1-4. The first place Alex should look is the agency contract or agency agreement. It specifies the scope of the agent's authority and relationship with the insurer.

Educational Objective 2

2-1. The insurance agent has the following responsibilities toward its principal, the insurer:
- Loyalty
- Obedience
- Reasonable care
- Accounting
- Relaying information

2-2. The insurer has the following responsibilities to its agents:
- Payment for services performed (commissions and other specified compensation to the agent for selling or renewing insurance)
- Indemnification (reimbursement) for losses or damages suffered without the agent's fault, but arising out of the agent's acts on behalf of the principal

2-3. If an insurance agent is told about a loss but fails to report it to the insurer, the insurer cannot deny its responsibility to pay the claim because agency law specifies that the insurer is presumed to know about any loss the agent knew about.

2-4. It could be argued that Ruth has violated the principal of reasonable care. The temporary employee should have had the appropriate credentials or background to perform the task of binding coverage. Given Kathie's lack of experience in insurance, Ruth should have coached her not to make commitments to customers and only to take telephone call messages.

Educational Objective 3

3-1. a. An example of an agent's express authority is selling the insurer's products or binding coverage.

   b. An example of an agent's implied authority is collecting premiums.

   c. An example of an agent's apparent authority is using insurer application blanks after the agency contract is terminated.

3-2. Carol, a licensed agent, can orally bind coverage and make insurance coverage protection effective immediately for a newly purchased car.

3-3. a. Yes, Radley would be obligated to pay a claim on the $200,000 policy even though the insurance agent is authorized to issue policies up to $100,000. Although Andy has exceeded his binding authority with Radley, Andy had apparent authority to issue the policy because the client could not be expected to know that Andy's binding authority was limited to $100,000.

   b. Radley would probably seek recovery in court from Andy for the cost of the claim, citing that he had exceeded his binding authority.

3-4. Yes, Don has insurance coverage on the contents of his apartment because oral binders are considered valid contracts of insurance. He does not need to possess the physical insurance policy to have coverage.

Educational Objective 4

4-1. Most insurers typically use one or more of the following marketing systems: independent agency system, exclusive agency system, direct writing system, or alternative distribution channels.

4-2. An insurance agency's expiration list is considered a valuable asset because the independent agency has an exclusive right to solicit policyholders on an agency expiration list and the right to sell its expiration list to another independent agent.

4-3. A producer in the direct writing system is an employee of the insurer. An exclusive agent is generally a self-employed representative of the company, not an employee of the insurer.

4-4. An exclusive agent can broker a customer's business through another agent who represents a different insurer to provide the customer with an unusual type of insurance.

4-5. The acquisition expenses avoided by an insurer's use of the direct response system are producer commissions.

4-6. Insurer XYZ uses the mixed marketing system; the company uses more than one marketing system or distribution channel (independent insurance agents and Internet).

4-7. a. Disagree. Even though an independent agent is not an employee of the insurer, the agent has express authority from the agency contract, implied authority from actions within its scope of authority, and apparent authority to act on behalf of the insurer. The insurer is required to honor the independent agent's commitments resulting from this authority.

   b. Agree. In representing several unrelated insurers, the independent agent can often select from the same insurance from different companies.

c. This may be true for some insurance customers, but not all. Direct mail insurance can have lower prices for the reasons Norma stated, but it is not necessarily the best deal for everyone. Many people prefer personal contact with a local agent who can provide additional and personalized services related to coverage needs, loss control, and claim settlement.

Educational Objective 5

5-1. a. When the insurer handles billing and premium collections (direct billing), the insurer periodically mails a commission check to the agency.

   b. When the agency collects the premiums (agency billing or producer billing), the agency subtracts its commission on each policy and remits the balance of collected premiums to the insurer, usually on a monthly basis.

5-2. a. An insurance agency must sell new policies or renew existing policies to receive sales commissions.

   b. An insurance agency must attain a certain volume of premium and a level of profitability to receive contingent commissions.

5-3. a. Services an agency provides before the insurance sale include locating and screening insurance prospects, conducting a successful sales solicitation, getting the necessary information to complete an application, preparing a submission to the insurer, and presenting a proposal or quote to the prospect.

   b. Services an agency provides after the insurance sale include handling the paperwork that accompanies policy changes, billing, and claim handling.

5-4. A contingent commission is based on the writing of profitable policies. XYZ may offer a high contingent commission for the sales volume of preferred homeowners policies written as long as they retain their profitability.

Educational Objective 6

6-1. a. When advertising, independent agencies attempt to attract customers for the agency, and local advertising often stresses the agency rather than the various insurers it represents.

   b. When advertising, many insurers marketing through the independent agency system use national advertising programs intended to enhance the company image. Advertising symbols are designed to increase public recognition of these insurers.

6-2. The advertising strategy used by producers' trade associations is intended to create a favorable image of members of the associations as a group and to make the public familiar with the logo and other symbols of each association.

6-3. [Different students may answer this question differently, depending on their own experiences.]
   - Advertising methods used by an insurer may include radio, television, and magazines in which national symbols or nationally advertised slogans are used.
   - An advertising method used by an agency may include the newspaper, which includes lists of agents and local offices, and descriptions of services, personnel, and reputation.

6-4. XYZ can create name brand recognition of the product so that customers will more readily accept the product when dealing with the agent.

Educational Objective 7

7-1. Ways insurers supervise their producers include the following:
- Sending marketing representatives to visit agents representing the insurer to develop and maintain sound working relationships with those agents and to motivate the agents to produce a satisfactory volume of profitable business for the insurer
- Sending production underwriters, who work in an insurer's office in an underwriting position, to visit agencies and clients to maintain rapport

7-2. To encourage insurance agents to sell their products, insurers provide the following:
- Personal relationships and encouragement (marketing representatives, regional managers)
- Marketing programs
- Financial incentives (salaries, bonuses, sales commissions, contingent commissions)
- Sales contests (recognition, prizes)

7-3. A home office marketing department cooperates with other departments to determine insurance coverage, price, and services based partly on claim costs for the particular insurer or for the industry as a whole and on information about the coverages, prices, and services of competing insurers.

7-4. The producers involved with the sales are probably the first to recognize the needed modifications of the small business product. XYZ may survey or meet with its producers to gather ideas about the problems that are not generating sales and solicit ideas for correcting those problems.

Educational Objective 8

8-1. State insurance departments regulate insurance producers' activities primarily through agent and broker licensing laws and other state laws dealing with insurance, such as unfair trade practices laws.

8-2. To obtain a state agent's license, a person must demonstrate knowledge of insurance principles and insurance laws and regulations by doing one of the following:
- Passing an examination and meeting other qualifications of the state insurance department
- Participating in classroom study
- Completing a recognized professional designation program

8-3. To retain a license, insurance producers must generally demonstrate continuing education by periodically completing a specified number of hours of educational study. Licensed producers are required to adhere to all state laws regulating insurance sales.

8-4. The purpose of educational and exam requirements is to set a base level of knowledge for those who will advise the public regarding insurance needs. Elimination of this knowledge base would not serve the public interest.

Educational Objective 9

9-1. Unfair trade practices that are prohibited for insurance producers include the following:
- Misrepresentation and false advertising
- Tie-in sales
- Rebating
- Other deceptive practices (for example, making a false statement about the financial condition of another insurer or putting false information on an insurance application)

9-2. It is an unfair trade practice for insurance agents or other insurance personnel to make, issue, or circulate information that does any of the following:
- Misrepresents the benefits, advantages, conditions, or terms of any insurance policy
- Misrepresents the dividends to be received on any insurance policy
- Makes false or misleading statements about dividends previously paid on any insurance policy
- Uses a name or title of insurance policies that misrepresents the true nature of the policies

9-3. Dean cannot coerce Patty to purchase insurance from XYZ Insurance Company because of the unfair trade practices law known as "tie-in sale." This law prohibits a producer from requiring that the purchase of insurance be tied to some other sale or financial arrangement.

9-4. Two behaviors that fall under the "other deceptive practices" category of the unfair trade practices laws are as follows:
- Insurers and their agents are prohibited from making a false statement about the financial condition of another insurer.
- Insurers and their agents are prohibited from putting false information on an insurance application to earn a commission from the insurance sale.

9-5. The policies did not cover all risks because some were excluded. The statement "all-risks" may have misrepresented the benefits or terms of the insurance policy and therefore could be considered misrepresentation or false advertising.

Direct Your Learning

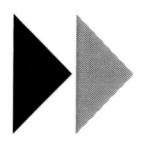

ASSIGNMENT 5

Underwriting

Educational Objectives

After learning the content of this assignment, you should be able to:

1. Describe the purpose of underwriting and an insurer's major underwriting activities to achieve that purpose.
2. Explain how underwriters protect an insurer's available capacity.
3. Explain which type of insurance rates would be more appropriate in a given situation:
   a. Class rates
   b. Individual rates
4. Describe the responsibilities of underwriting management.
5. Describe the steps in the underwriting process that an underwriter follows in selecting policyholders.
6. Describe information sources that underwriters use in the underwriting process.
7. Describe four categories of hazards that underwriters must evaluate in reviewing an application for insurance.
8. Describe an underwriter's options when evaluating an application for insurance.
9. Explain how states regulate underwriting activities through restrictions on unfair discrimination, cancellation, and nonrenewal.
10. Define or describe each of the Key Words and Phrases for this assignment.

Study Materials

Required Reading:
- Property and Liability Insurance Principles
  - Chapter 5

Study Aids:
- SMART Online Practice Exams
- SMART Study Aids
  - Review Notes and Flash Cards—Assignment 5

Outline

- **Underwriting Activities**
  - A. Selecting Insureds
    1. Adverse Selection Considerations
    2. Capacity Considerations
  - B. Pricing Coverage
    1. Premium Determination
    2. Class Rates
    3. Individual Rates
  - C. Determining Policy Terms and Conditions
  - D. Monitoring Underwriting Decisions
- **Underwriting Management**
  - A. Participating in Insurer Management
  - B. Arranging Reinsurance
  - C. Delegating Underwriting Authority
  - D. Developing and Enforcing Underwriting Guidelines
  - E. Monitoring Underwriting Results
- **The Underwriting Process**
  - A. Gathering Underwriting Information
  - B. Making the Underwriting Decision
    1. Analyzing Hazards
    2. Evaluating Underwriting Options
  - C. Implementing the Underwriting Decision
  - D. Monitoring the Underwriting Decision
- **Regulation of Underwriting Activities**
  - A. Prohibition of Unfair Discrimination
  - B. Restrictions on Cancellation and Nonrenewal
- **Summary**

s.m.a.r.t. tips
The SMART Online Practice Exams product contains a final practice exam. You should take this exam only when you have completed your study of the entire course. It will be your best indicator of how well prepared you are.

Underwriting 5.3

For each assignment, you should define or describe each of the Key Words and Phrases and answer each of the Review and Application Questions.

Educational Objective 1
Describe the purpose of underwriting and an insurer's major underwriting activities to achieve that purpose.

Key Words and Phrases

Underwriting (p. 5.3)

Underwriter (p. 5.3)

Adverse selection (p. 5.4)

Review Questions

1-1. List the four activities in the underwriting process.
(p. 5.3)

1-2. How do underwriters avoid the effects of adverse selection?
(p. 5.4)

Application Question

1-3. Statistics show that the occupants of small vehicles involved in collisions with larger vehicles sustain more injuries than the occupants in the larger vehicles. XYZ Insurance Company has noticed a trend in its automobile applications over the past year: applicants with large vehicles and heavy pickup trucks are requesting higher limits of liability coverage to pay for injuries that they may cause to others. Explain whether this is an example of adverse selection. (p. 5.4)

Educational Objective 2
Explain how underwriters protect an insurer's available capacity.

Key Word or Phrase
Capacity (p. 5.4)

Review Questions

2-1. Every insurer has a limited capacity to accept business. (pp. 5.4–5.6)

   a. Why is each insurer's capacity limited?

   b. How do insurers protect their available capacity?

2-2. Why do insurers maintain a spread of risk, and how do they do it? (p. 5.5)

2-3. How does reinsurance help a primary insurer to write more business than it could handle without reinsurance? (pp. 5.5–5.6)

Educational Objective 3
Explain which type of insurance rates would be more appropriate in a given situation:
a. Class rates
b. Individual rates

Key Words and Phrases

Class rate, or manual rate (p. 5.7)

Merit rating plan (p. 5.7)

Individual rate, or specific rate (p. 5.8)

Judgment rate (p. 5.8)

Standard form (p. 5.8)

Hazard (p. 5.9)

Book of business, or portfolio (p. 5.9)

Review Questions

3-1. Give four examples of ways in which merit rating plans can modify class rates. (pp. 5.7–5.8)

3-2. Under what circumstances are individual rates used rather than class rates? (p. 5.8)

3-3. In what situations are judgment rates used? (p. 5.8)

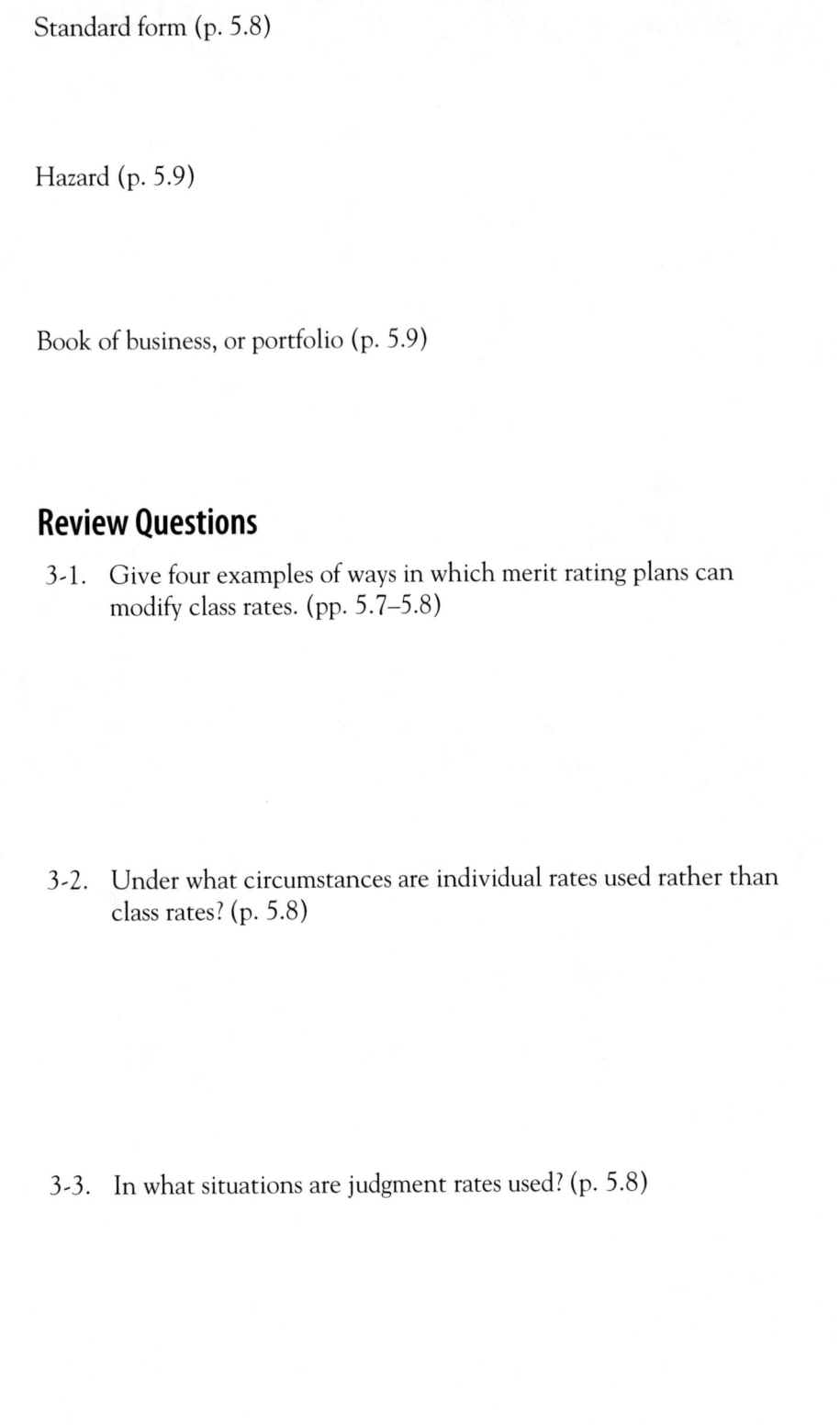

Application Questions

3-4. Clarence, an insurer underwriting supervisor, explains to a new employee that the insurer does not write property insurance on frame buildings located where there are no fire hydrants because the insurer would not be able to charge a premium commensurate with the loss exposure. Explain Clarence's statement in your own words. (p. 5.6)

3-5. Radley Insurance Company has decided to offer a unique insurance policy to cover golf carts and golf equipment in retirement and golfing communities. Explain whether the rates that Radley develops for this new policy are apt to be class rates or individual rates. (pp. 5.7–5.8)

Educational Objective 4
Describe the responsibilities of underwriting management.

Key Words and Phrases
Treaty reinsurance (p. 5.10)

Facultative reinsurance (p. 5.11)

Underwriting authority (p. 5.11)

Underwriting audit (p. 5.12)

Review Questions

4-1. What responsibilities are met by underwriting management? (p. 5.10)

4-2. What is the distinction between treaty reinsurance and facultative reinsurance? (pp. 5.10–5.11)

4-3. Underwriting management develops, enforces, and monitors underwriting guidelines. (pp. 5.11–5.12)

   a. Why is it necessary for underwriting management to monitor underwriting guidelines?

   b. What is the purpose of an underwriting audit?

Application Question

4-4. Spring Insurance Company is interested in limiting its maximum property loss on any homeowners policy to $250,000. However, many of the homes on new applications are valued above that amount. Would treaty reinsurance or facultative reinsurance be helpful to Spring in this particular situation? Explain. (pp. 5.10–5.11)

Educational Objective 5
Describe the steps in the underwriting process that an underwriter follows in selecting policyholders.

Key Word or Phrase
Expert systems, or knowledge-based systems (p. 5.13)

Review Questions

5-1. Identify the steps in the underwriting process. (p. 5.12)

5-2. Describe "computerized underwriting processes," and identify the types of insurance with which it is most common. (pp. 5.12–5.13)

5-3. Does an expert system replace the need for underwriters? (p. 5.13)

Application Question

5-4. An agent at the Atwell Agency has completed an application for insurance on a garden shop. The agent sends the application to XYZ Insurance Company to be underwritten. Describe the steps the underwriter would go through in underwriting the garden shop's application. (pp. 5.12–5.13)

Educational Objective 6
Describe information sources that underwriters use in the underwriting process.

Review Questions

6-1. Underwriters obtain underwriting information from many sources. List four sources and describe the type(s) of information available from each. (pp. 5.13–5.14)

6-2. What duties does a loss control representative perform when creating an inspection report? (p. 5.14)

6-3. What duties does a premium auditor perform when creating a premium audit report? (p. 5.14)

Application Question

6-4. Consider your own house or apartment, or the house or apartment of a friend or family member. When the insurance policy was written covering the structure and contents of the house or the contents of the apartment, an underwriter made a decision regarding the sources of information that he or she would use in deciding whether to write the policy that covers that property. Describe how the underwriter might have used information from the insured's records. (p. 5.14)

Educational Objective 7

Describe four categories of hazards that underwriters must evaluate in reviewing an application for insurance.

Key Words and Phrases

Moral hazard (p. 5.15)

Attitudinal hazard, or morale hazard (p. 5.15)

Physical hazard (p. 5.16)

Legal hazard (p. 5.16)

Review Questions

7-1. What are the four categories of hazards? (p. 5.15)

7-2. What is the distinction between moral hazards and attitudinal (morale) hazards? (p. 5.15)

7-3. Give at least one example of each of the following: (p. 5.16)

   a. Physical hazards

   b. Legal hazards

Application Questions

7-4. Anne, an underwriter, has been asked to provide liability insurance for the owner of a fifty-year-old office building in run-down condition. What types of hazards may Anne need to consider in evaluating this risk? (pp. 5.15–5.16)

7-5. The houses constructed in Historic community are generally over 200 years old and in excellent condition. The covenants in the community are strictly enforced by an architectural review committee that requires homes to be reconstructed to their original state if they are damaged or if they deteriorate. Many insurers are reluctant to write insurance for the homes in this area because the premiums are not commensurate with the loss exposures presented by the hand-carved woodwork and the slate roofs on these homes. Insurers would have to replace these features, an expense that often exceeds the market value of the homes. Insurers are often unwilling to insure homes for a value that is greatly in excess of their market value. Describe the type of hazard this case demonstrates. (pp. 5.15–5.16)

Educational Objective 8
Describe an underwriter's options when evaluating an application for insurance.

Review Questions

8-1. What underwriting options are available besides accepting or rejecting an application as submitted? (pp. 5.16–5.17)

8-2. Describe the steps an underwriter follows when implementing an underwriting decision for a complex case. (p. 5.17)

8-3. What corrective action can an underwriter take if serious problems develop with an account? (p. 5.18)

Application Question

8-4. Alfred, an underwriter, has received a homeowners application for a property that has experienced a number of claims in the past three years. These claims have all involved property that was taken from the applicant's yard. None of the losses exceeded $300. Alfred is considering accepting the application with modification. Suggest modifications that may make the application more acceptable. (pp. 5.16–5.17)

Educational Objective 9

Explain how states regulate underwriting activities through restrictions on unfair discrimination, cancellation, and nonrenewal.

Review Questions

9-1. What is the difference between fair discrimination and unfair discrimination in insurance underwriting? (pp. 5.19–5.20)

9-2. List three examples of unfair discrimination. (pp. 5.19–5.20)

9-3. What restrictions may be placed on underwriters' rights to cancel or nonrenew insurance policies? (p. 5.20)

Application Question

9-4. XYZ Insurance Company has experienced excessive theft, vandalism, and suspicious fire losses in one territory. Upon investigation, the underwriters discovered that the major employer in the territory had closed. The resulting unemployment has created financial pressures on many former workers. It is suspected that the losses are a result of these pressures. XYZ has implemented a significant rate increase for all property in this territory as a result of the losses. Judge whether the rate increase implemented by XYZ is an example of fair or unfair discrimination. (pp. 5.19–5.20)

Answers to Assignment 5 Questions

NOTE: These answers are provided to give students a basic understanding of acceptable types of responses. They often are not the only valid answers and are not intended to provide an exhaustive response to the questions.

Educational Objective 1

1-1. The four activities in the underwriting process include the following:
- Selecting insureds—The insurer screens applicants to determine which ones it desires to insure.
- Pricing coverage—The insurer charges a premium commensurate with the loss exposure and adequate to pay the losses and expenses for the group and to allow the insurer to achieve a reasonable profit or gain.
- Determining policy terms and conditions—The insurer decides exactly what types of coverage will be provided to each applicant.
- Monitoring underwriting decisions—The insurer examines the hazards, loss experience, and other conditions of specific insureds or examines an insurer's entire book of business to determine whether any significant changes have occurred.

1-2. Underwriters avoid the effects of adverse selection by screening applicants to identify, and decline coverage to, those who present loss potentials that would be inadequately reflected in the rates.

1-3. This may be an example of adverse selection: people with the greatest probability of increased losses are purchasing higher limits of coverage. However, adverse selection normally occurs if the premium is low relative to the loss exposures. This example may simply be the case of applicants who have purchased larger, and presumably more expensive, vehicles also choosing to purchase additional limits of coverage because it is affordable to them.

Educational Objective 2

2-1. a. Each insurer's capacity to accept business is limited because putting new business on the books creates upfront expenses, and the amount of money an insurer can afford to invest in new business is limited by the insurer's policyholders' surplus.
   b. Insurers protect their available capacity in the following ways:
   - Maintain a spread of risk
   - Optimize the use of available resources
   - Arrange for reinsurance

2-2. Insurers spread their risk among various types of insurance with exposures in different geographic areas. This practice reduces the chance that overall underwriting results will be adversely affected by a large number of losses in any one type of insurance or any one territory.

2-3. Reinsurance helps a primary insurer increase its capacity to write business by transferring some of the premium and financial consequences of loss exposures to reinsurers.

Educational Objective 3

3-1. Merit rating plans can modify class rates in the following ways:
- A safe driver insurance plan (personal auto insurance) lowers the premiums for drivers with a history of accident-free driving and no major traffic convictions.
- A premium discount (homeowners insurance) lowers the premiums for insureds with fire alarms or burglar alarms.
- An experience rating (commercial insurance) increases premiums for insureds whose loss experience has been worse than average and decreases premiums for insureds whose loss experience has been better than average.
- A schedule rating (commercial insurance) lists credits or debits based on certain characteristics not reflected in the class rate.

3-2. Individual rates rather than class rates are used for commercial property insurance on unique structures to reflect the following characteristics of the building:
- Construction
- Occupancy
- Public and private fire protection
- External exposures

3-3. Judgment rates are used for ocean marine insurance covering many types of cargo transported worldwide. Judgment rates are also used for one-of-a-kind exposures.

3-4. A premium commensurate with the loss exposure would mean that the insurer could not charge enough money to cover the very high risk for an applicant who has hazards much greater than those assumed when rates are established.

3-5. Radley will probably use class rates. Although this is a unique insurance policy, the loss exposures for golf carts and golf equipment are fairly uniform. These loss exposures could be grouped into rating classes.

Educational Objective 4

4-1. The responsibilities of an insurer's underwriting management include the following:
- Participating in the insurer's overall management
- Arranging reinsurance
- Delegating underwriting authority
- Developing and enforcing underwriting guidelines
- Monitoring underwriting results

4-2. The distinction between treaty reinsurance and facultative reinsurance is that treaty reinsurance automatically reinsures all eligible policies while facultative reinsurance involves a separate transaction for each reinsured policy.

4-3. a. Underwriting management monitors underwriting results to see whether the underwriting guidelines have the desired effect of guiding underwriters toward consistent decisions that enable the insurer to meet its overall underwriting objectives.

b. Underwriting management uses an underwriting audit to determine whether underwriters are following the underwriting guidelines.

4-4. In the likeliest scenario, Spring would arrange for treaty reinsurance by which a reinsurer would automatically assume all property losses exceeding $250,000 on any homeowners policy. In theory, Spring could buy facultative reinsurance for each instance, but this would be cumbersome and carry a high transaction cost.

Educational Objective 5

5-1. The steps in the underwriting process include the following:
- Gathering underwriting information
- Making the underwriting decision
- Implementing that decision
- Monitoring the underwriting decision

5-2. Computerized underwriting processes use software that emulates the steps an underwriter would take. The computer screens applications and accepts those that clearly meet all criteria and rejects those that clearly do not. Computerized underwriting is most common with high-volume types of insurance such as personal auto or homeowners insurance.

5-3. Although expert underwriting systems are capable of making an underwriting decision, most are used to supplement an underwriter's decision making, not to replace the underwriter.

5-4. The underwriter would gather underwriting information using a variety of sources. The underwriter would then analyze the information to determine what hazards the garden shop represents, including physical hazards, legal hazards, and possible moral and attitudinal hazards. Then the underwriter would identify underwriting options, choose the best option, implement that decision, and monitor that decision periodically.

Educational Objective 6

6-1. Answers may vary; four sources used by an underwriter to obtain underwriting information include the following:
- Consumer investigation reports that contain background information on prospective insureds
- Financial rating services that provide data on the credit rating and financial stability of specific businesses
- Production records that provide a track record of the producer who submits the application
- Government records such as motor vehicle records and court records that may yield useful information for auto or property insurance underwriting

Other sources that may be included in the answer are: producers, inspection reports, field marketing personnel, claim files, premium audit reports, and the applicant's or insured's records.

6-2. When creating an inspection report, a loss control representative's duties include inspecting the premises and operations of insurance applicants and preparing reports for underwriters.

6-3. When creating a premium audit report, a premium auditor obtains the final figures from insureds' accounting records to compute the final premium on commercial insurance policies. In addition, the premium auditor provides other information about the insured, especially because the premium auditor has probably visited the insured's premises and seen the operations.

6-4. The underwriter might have reviewed the applicant's or insured's records such as copies of appraisals of jewelry and bills of sale.

Educational Objective 7

7-1. The four categories of hazards are moral hazards, attitudinal (morale) hazards, physical hazards, and legal hazards.

7-2. • Someone who represents a moral hazard may intentionally cause a loss or file a false claim.
 • Someone who represents an attitudinal (morale) hazard may be careless in causing a loss.

7-3. a. Examples of physical hazards include a restaurant without adequate fire protection located next to an office building and in an area without fire hydrants.
 b. Examples of legal hazards include court decisions interpreting policy language in a way unfavorable to insurers and state regulation restricting insurers' ability to cancel or nonrenew policies.

7-4. In evaluating risk of providing liability insurance for the owner of a fifty-year-old building in run-down condition, Anne may consider the following:
 • Physical hazards, including the building's construction, other occupants of the building, types of fire protection, and external exposures
 • Moral hazards, which include dishonest tendencies of the insured, its occupants, or employees
 • Attitudinal (morale) hazards, which include poor management (tolerance of run-down condition), past loss experience, housekeeping, maintenance, and carelessness because of insurance coverage

7-5. This case demonstrates a legal hazard. The covenants of the community create an environment in which the insurer cannot provide insurance with appropriate premiums.

Educational Objective 8

8-1. Underwriting options available to an underwriter besides accepting or rejecting an application as submitted are to accept the application with modification such as the following:
 • Having the applicant agree to implement loss control measures
 • Modifying the rate charged for the coverage
 • Modifying some aspect of the coverage by offering different terms and conditions
 • Seeking reinsurance if the application exceeds the limit in the underwriting guidelines

8-2. When implementing an underwriting decision for a complex case, an underwriter must communicate his or her decision to the producer, along with a quote showing the premium to be charged and the terms and conditions to be offered.

8-3. If serious problems develop with an account, an underwriter may recommend additional loss control measures, modify the terms of coverage, cancel coverage (if permitted), or mark the policy for nonrenewal at the end of the present policy term.

8-4. Alfred may do one or more of the following:
- Require the insured to secure the yard with a gated fence
- Accept the application as a standard class or reduced class risk
- Increase the policy deductible to cover the losses, such as $500

Educational Objective 9

9-1. Insurance underwriting strives for fair discrimination by applying the same standard or method of treatment to insureds—distinguishing among properties, businesses, and people; grouping them into categories; and charging a premium commensurate with their loss exposures. Unfair discrimination involves applying different standards or methods of treatment to insureds who have the same basic characteristics and loss potential.

9-2. Three examples of unfair discrimination include refusing to issue, cancel, or nonrenew coverage for an applicant or an insured solely on the basis of the applicant's or insured's geographic location (sometimes called "redlining"), gender or marital status, or race.

9-3. The restrictions that may be placed on underwriters' rights to cancel or nonrenew insurance policies are as follows:
- Requiring insurers to notify the insured within a specified period before a policy is to be canceled or nonrenewed
- Prohibiting insurers from canceling insurance policies during the policy term and restricting insurers' rights to nonrenew policies

9-4. Although not all of XYZ's property policyholders in the territory would view it as fair, the action by XYZ is an example of fair discrimination. The premium increase charged was commensurate with the increased loss exposures experienced by the property owners in the territory.

Direct Your Learning

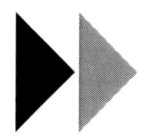

Claims

Educational Objectives

After learning the content of this assignment, you should be able to:

1. Describe the role performed by each of the following in the claim handling process:

    a. Staff claim representatives (inside and outside)

    b. Independent adjusters

    c. Producers

    d. Public adjusters

2. Describe the activities in the claim handling process.

3. Describe how the claim handling process applies to property insurance claims.

4. Describe how the claim handling process applies to liability insurance claims.

5. Describe the special considerations for catastrophe claims.

6. Describe the claim representative's role in establishing an insurer's loss reserves.

7. Describe the practices prohibited by unfair claim practices laws.

8. Define or describe each of the Key Words and Phrases for this assignment.

ASSIGNMENT 6

Study Materials

Required Reading:
- Property and Liability Insurance Principles
  - Chapter 6

Study Aids:
- SMART Online Practice Exams
- SMART Study Aids
  - Review Notes and Flash Cards—Assignment 6

Outline

- **Claim Handling Responsibility**
    - A. Staff Claim Representatives of Insurers
        1. Inside Claim Representatives
        2. Outside Claim Representatives
    - B. Independent Adjusters
    - C. Producers
    - D. Public Adjusters
    - E. Claim Handling Under Self-Insurance Plans
        1. Internal Claim Departments
        2. Third-Party Administrators
- **Claim Handling Process**
    - A. Property Insurance Claims
        1. Verifying Coverage
        2. Determining the Cause of Loss
        3. Determining the Amount of Damages or Extent of Loss
        4. Negotiating and Settling the Claim
    - B. Subrogation and Salvage Rights
    - C. Liability Insurance Claims
        1. Verifying Coverage
        2. Determining the Cause of Loss
        3. Valuation
        4. Negotiating and Settling the Claim
- **Special Considerations for Catastrophe Claims**
    - A. Processing the Increased Number of Property Claims
    - B. Dealing With Claim Handling Scrutiny
- **Loss Reserves**
- **Unfair Claim Practices Laws**
- **Summary**

When you take the randomized full practice exams in the SMART Online Practice Exams product, you are seeing the same kinds of questions you will see when you take the actual exam. Take advantage of your time and learn the features of the software now.

Claims 6.3

For each assignment, you should define or describe each of the Key Words and Phrases and answer each of the Review and Application Questions.

> ## Educational Objective 1
> Describe the role performed by each of the following in the claim handling process:
> a. Staff claim representatives (inside and outside)
> b. Independent adjusters
> c. Agents
> d. Public adjusters

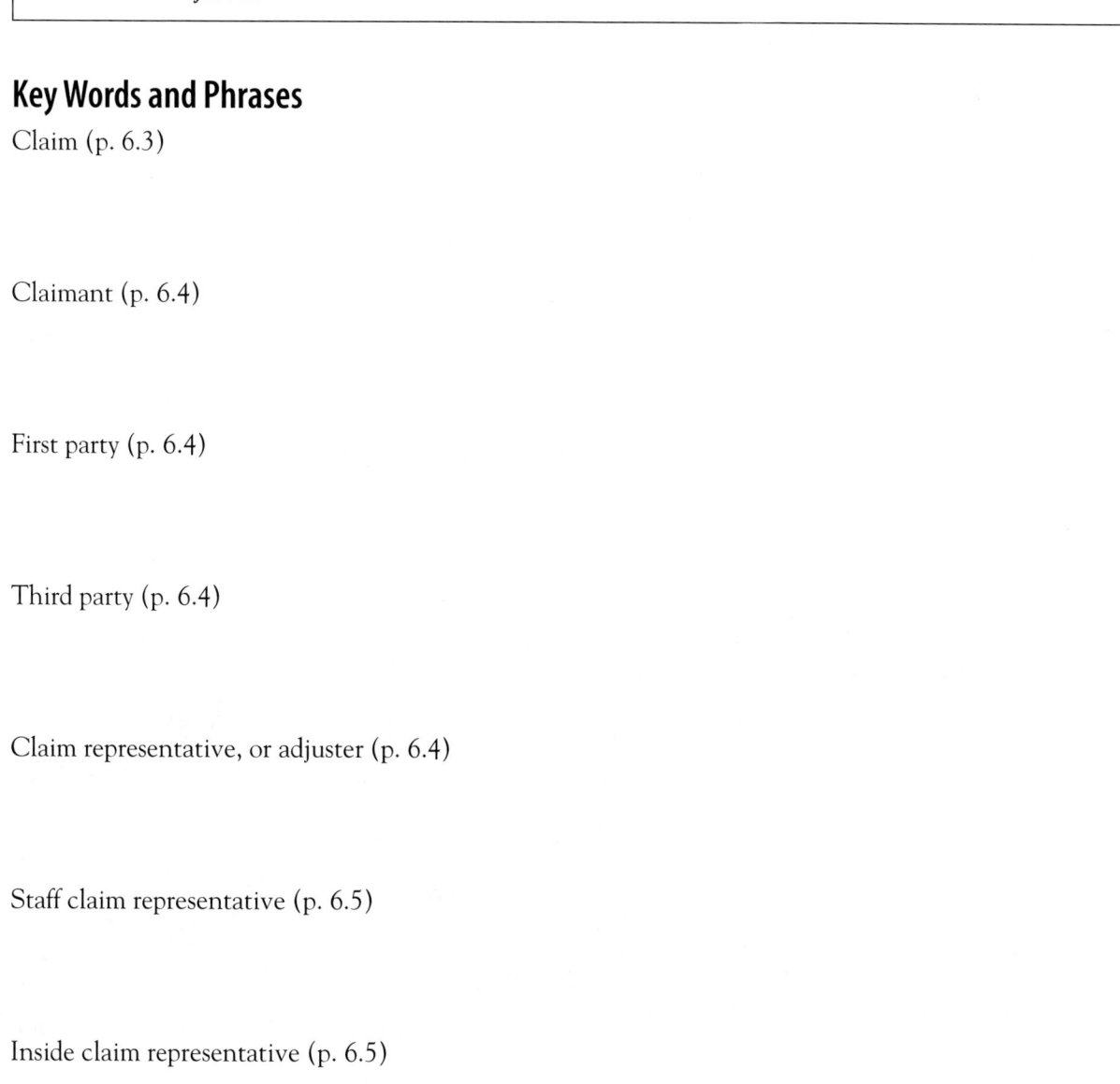

Key Words and Phrases

Claim (p. 6.3)

Claimant (p. 6.4)

First party (p. 6.4)

Third party (p. 6.4)

Claim representative, or adjuster (p. 6.4)

Staff claim representative (p. 6.5)

Inside claim representative (p. 6.5)

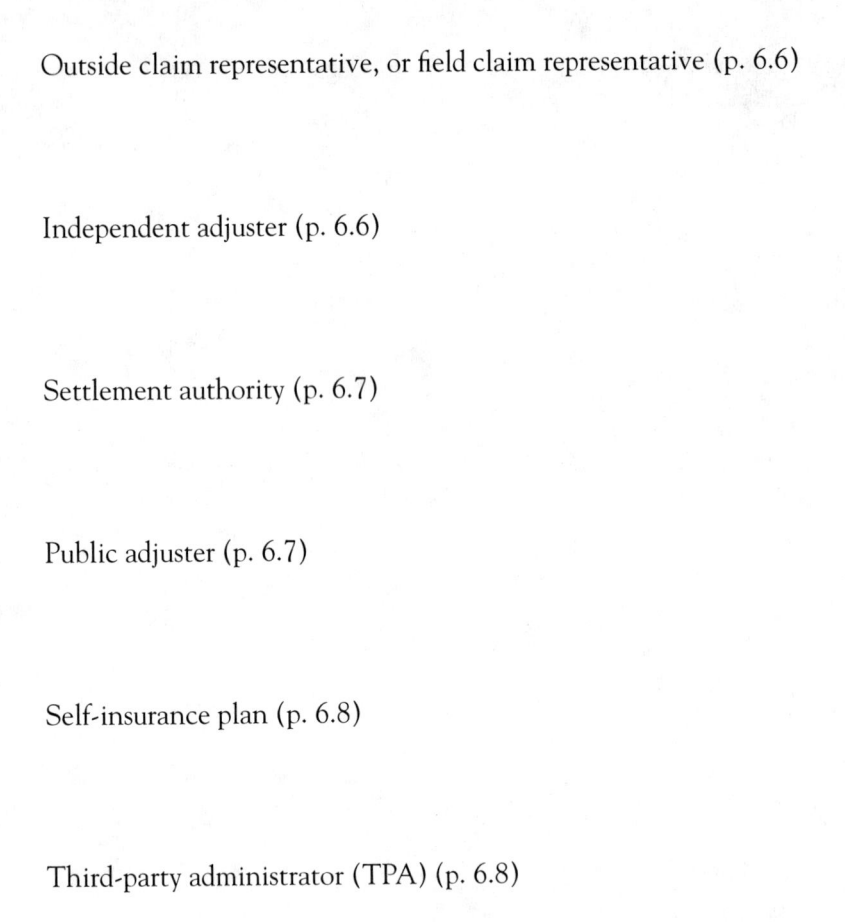

Outside claim representative, or field claim representative (p. 6.6)

Independent adjuster (p. 6.6)

Settlement authority (p. 6.7)

Public adjuster (p. 6.7)

Self-insurance plan (p. 6.8)

Third-party administrator (TPA) (p. 6.8)

Review Questions

1-1. In handling a claim, what are the responsibilities of a claim representative? (pp. 6.4–6.5)

1-2. Although one frequently hears the terms "first party" and "third party," the "second party" to an insurance contract is rarely mentioned. Identify each of the "three parties" involved in an insurance contract. (p. 6.4)

   a. The first party

   b. The second party

   c. The third party

1-3. Under what circumstances would a claim most likely be handled by each of the following? (pp. 6.5–6.9)

   a. Inside claim representative

   b. Outside claim representative

c. Producer

d. Insured's internal claim department

e. Third-party administrator (TPA)

1-4. Describe two situations in which an insurer may hire an independent adjuster. (pp. 6.6–6.7)

1-5. A public adjuster does not handle claims on behalf of an insurer. What is the role of a public adjuster? (pp. 6.7–6.8)

Application Question

1-6. Ralph is the claim manager for a small mutual insurer located on the Gulf Coast. Ralph has a team of outside claim representatives to handle the property losses that normally occur. However, Ralph is preparing a contingency plan in the event that a hurricane passes along the Gulf Coast and damages a significant number of businesses and homes that his company insures. There are not enough outside claim representatives to handle a large number of claims in a timely fashion. Explain how Ralph could use individuals in other roles to help with the claim handling process in a time of crisis. (pp. 6.6–6.8)

Educational Objective 2

Describe the activities in the claim handling process.

Review Questions

2-1. Illustrate how claim handling procedures can vary between a minor, single-vehicle auto accident and an accident involving two or more autos. (p. 6.9)

2-2. What are the four steps involved in processing claims? (p. 6.9)

> **Educational Objective 3**
> Describe how the claim handling process applies to property insurance claims.

Key Words and Phrases

Reservation of rights letter (p. 6.10)

Insurable interest (p. 6.10)

Actual cash value (ACV) (p. 6.14)

Depreciation (p. 6.14)

Replacement cost (p. 6.14)

Agreed value (p. 6.14)

Subrogation (p. 6.17)

Salvage rights (p. 6.17)

Constructive total loss (p. 6.17)

Review Questions

3-1. Under what circumstances might a claim representative use a reservation of rights letter? (p. 6.10)

3-2. Describe each of the following steps for property insurance claims. (pp. 6.10–6.18)

   a. Verifying coverage

   b. Determining the cause of loss

   c. Determining the amount of damages or extent of loss

   d. Negotiating and settling the claim

3-3. Depending on policy provisions, property losses may be valued on an actual cash value basis, a replacement cost basis, or an agreed value basis. (pp. 6.14–6.15)

   a. Explain the relevance, if any, of depreciation to each of the three valuation methods mentioned above.

   b. A fifteen-year-old sofa, insured for its actual cash value, is destroyed in a house fire. The claim representative finds that the destroyed sofa was of a type that is usually considered to have a "useful life" of ten years. Does this mean that the insurer will not need to pay anything for the destroyed sofa? Explain.

3-4. Connie ran a red light and collided with Klaus's car, damaging it to the extent that repairs would cost more than the car was worth. (p. 6.17)

   a. Was Klaus's car a constructive total loss? Explain.

   b. Explain how both subrogation and salvage rights would probably be involved in handling Klaus's claim. (p. 6.17)

Application Questions

3-5. Sarah is a claim representative who handles collision damage claims for personal automobiles. Lisa, when reporting her recent accident, pressured Sarah to settle the loss quickly. Lisa said that she would be willing to take $2,000 if Sarah would just write a check for her that day. It was obvious that the vehicle was worth at least twice that amount. Explain if Sarah would or would not be able to comply with Lisa's request. (pp. 6.13–6.14)

3-6. Raymond, a claim representative, was assigned a claim involving a break-in at a business and theft of property from the insured premises. The police report indicated that the window at the premises had been broken from the inside, but there was no other source of damage to indicate how any thief had entered the premises. Raymond has decided to do further investigation to obtain more information about the break-in. Describe the action Raymond must take to protect his company's right to later deny the claim if the claim is found to be fraudulent. (p. 6.10)

Educational Objective 4
Describe how the claim handling process applies to liability insurance claims.

Key Words and Phrases
Damages (p. 6.19)

Compensatory damages (p. 6.19)

Special damages (p. 6.20)

General damages (p. 6.20)

Punitive damages (p. 6.20)

Review Questions

4-1. Identify the four processes involved in claim handling for liability insurance claims. (pp. 6.18–6.21)

4-2. For liability claim handling, what is the key difference from property claims? (pp. 6.17–6.18)

4-3. Under what circumstances might a liability claim result in no payment of damages? (pp. 6.18–6.20)

4-4. Are most liability claims settled by a lawsuit? Explain. (pp. 6.20–6.21)

Application Question

4-5. Charlotte was severely injured when the new ladder that she had purchased collapsed while she was cleaning the gutter on her house. Investigation revealed that the ladder had been improperly constructed. The manufacturer was aware of the defect and had received multiple complaints about the problem. Charlotte sued the ladder manufacturer and received the following for her injuries:

- $300,500 for her hospital bills and rehabilitation
- $30,000 for her lost wages
- $500,000 for loss of use of her left hand and scarring to her arm
- $750,000 awarded as punishment against the ladder manufacturer for careless disregard for the safety of its customers

Categorize each bulleted item according to the type of damages it represents. (p. 6.20)

Educational Objective 5
Describe the special considerations for catastrophe claims.

Review Questions

5-1. Describe the two primary sources of activity for insurers processing losses that originate in a catastrophe. (pp. 6.21–6.23)

5-2. What purposes are served by an insurer's developing contingency plans before a catastrophe hits? (p. 6.21)

Application Question

5-3. The Callaway Insurance Company insures many coastal homes in Georgia, Florida, and Louisiana. During one particularly severe hurricane season, there were three catastrophic events that affected the policyholders of Callaway. In a period of two weeks, claim volume was five times higher than normal. In response, Callaway's management suspended the claim settlement authority of producers so that all claimants would deal with a Callaway employee. Callaway also added some new survey and checklist forms to its claim handling procedures to help ensure that all catastrophe victims received fair treatment. Finally, Callaway authorized advance payments to policyholders who needed additional living expenses because of property loss. Which of these actions would you have recommended? (p. 6.23)

Educational Objective 6

Describe the claim representative's role in establishing an insurer's loss reserves.

Key Word or Phrase

Case reserve (p. 6.24)

Review Questions

6-1. Why are claim representatives required to establish loss reserves on claims that have occurred but have not yet been settled? (pp. 6.23–6.24)

6-2. What is a case reserve? (p. 6.24)

6-3. Who calculates an insurer's overall loss reserves? What role do case reserves have in the determination of overall loss reserves? (p. 6.24)

Application Question

6-4. James had an automobile accident on January 13, which he reported to his insurance agent three days later, on January 16. Because several people were injured, James's insurer, XYZ Insurance Company, established an initial loss reserve of $200,000. (pp. 6.23–6.25)

   a. Explain what a loss reserve is and why XYZ established a reserve for James's claim.

   b. Explain how the loss reserve could change as this claim passes through its various stages.

Educational Objective 7
Describe the practices prohibited by unfair claim practices laws.

Key Word or Phrase
Unfair claim practices law (p. 6.25)

Review Questions

7-1. Identify two misconceptions a claimant may have about a claim representative. (p. 6.25)

7-2. What claim practices are prohibited by unfair claim practices laws? (pp. 6.25)

7-3. Identify the repercussions a claim representative or insurer may face if they cannot justify claim practices that are under scrutiny. (p. 6.26)

Application Question

7-4. Jacob was injured in an automobile accident. He was stopped at a red light when the pickup truck behind him, driven by Bill, ran into him. The police report charged Bill with causing the accident. Jacob has attempted to contact Bill's insurer for two months without success. He has received telephone messages from the claim representative informing him that the claim representative has been unable to contact Bill to obtain his statement. The claim representative advised Jacob to go to his own insurer to arrange to have repairs made to his car and to see if there is any coverage for Jacob's injuries. Analyze this case and describe those elements that may indicate violations of the unfair claim practices laws. (p. 6.25)

Answers to Assignment 6 Questions

NOTE: These answers are provided to give students a basic understanding of acceptable types of responses. They often are not the only valid answers and are not intended to provide an exhaustive response to the questions.

Educational Objective 1

1-1. The responsibilities of the claim representative when handling a claim include the following:
- Verify coverage
- Determine the cause of loss
- Determine the amount of damages or extent of loss
- Negotiate and/or settle the claim

1-2. a. The insured is the first party involved in an insurance contract.
   b. The insurer is the second party involved in an insurance contract.
   c. The claimant is the third party involved in an insurance contract.

1-3. a. A claim that would most likely be handled by an inside claim representative is a relatively simple claim that can be settled by telephone or letter from inside the insurer's office.
   b. A claim that would most likely be handled by an outside claim representative is a claim that cannot be handled easily by phone or mail and may involve a visit to the scene of a loss, an interview with witnesses, an investigation of damage, or a meeting with persons involved with the claim.
   c. A claim that would most likely be handled by producer is a relatively small claim.
   d. A claim that would most likely be handled by an insured's internal claim department would be that of a large organization with a self-insurance plan and an internal claim department.
   e. A claim that would most likely be handled by a third-party administrator (TPA) would be that of an organization that has a self-insurance plan but not an internal claim department.

1-4. An insurer may hire an independent adjuster if a claim involves a unique or complex situation and the staff claim representative does not have sufficient expertise to handle the claim. Examples of such claims would involve business income or ocean marine insurance. Another situation in which an insurer may hire an independent adjuster is after a natural disaster, such as a severe hurricane. Because of the volume of claims generated by natural disasters, insurers not only send staff claim representatives to work with insureds, but also hire independent adjusters to assist in handling claims.

1-5. The role of a public adjuster is to represent the insured in handling a claim.

1-6. Ralph could do any or all of the following:
- Contract independent adjusters who would adjust those claims that his staff is unable to handle.
- Expand settlement authority to producers following a crisis so that they would settle more claims on behalf of the insurer.
- Train existing staff members to be inside claim representatives to gather information concerning claims and to settle relatively simple cases during the crisis.

Educational Objective 2

2-1. The claim handling procedures for a minor, single-vehicle auto accident include verifying coverage, obtaining estimates of the damage to the automobile, and paying the claim. For an accident involving two or more autos, those involved in the accident may provide conflicting testimony about the events surrounding the accident. Difficult questions about legal liability may arise, and the claim representative may need the perspective of a physician, a lawyer, an engineer, and a police officer to understand all of the issues.

2-2. The four steps in processing claims include the following:
- Verifying coverage
- Determining the cause of loss
- Determining the amount of damages or extent of loss
- Negotiating and settling (or denying) the claim

Educational Objective 3

3-1. A claim representative might use a reservation of rights letter when a question of coverage exists and the insurer wishes to continue its investigation while reserving its rights to deny coverage later.

3-2. a. Coverage is verified by determining whether an insurable interest exists, whether the policy covers the damaged property, whether the policy covers the cause of loss, and whether any additional coverages, endorsements, or coverage limitations apply.

b. Determining the cause of loss may involve a visit to the loss site or interviews of witnesses to the loss.

c. Determining the amount of damages or extent of loss depends on whether the valuation procedure specifies actual cash value, replacement cost, agreed value, or some other valuation method.

d. After completing coverage verification, cause of loss determination, and loss valuation, the claim representative negotiates and settles the claim with the insured.

3-3. a. When property is insured for its actual cash value, depreciation can affect the amount of recovery for any loss. That is because actual cash value is determined by deducting the amount of depreciation on an item of lost property from what it would cost to replace the item with new property. Depreciation does not enter into recovery on a replacement cost basis, because replacement cost coverage pays the full cost of replacing lost property. Depreciation also does not apply to total loss of property covered on an agreed value basis, because a valued policy pays the agreed amount stated in the policy, regardless of the property's actual value at time of loss.

b. Although the sofa destroyed in the fire was older than its useful life, useful life is only an estimate or an average and may or may not be accurate in a particular loss. If the sofa still had some functional value at the time of loss, the insurer probably would recognize that value and attempt to compensate the insured fairly.

3-4. a. Yes. A constructive total loss exists because Klaus's car cannot be repaired for less than the car is worth.

b. Both subrogation and salvage rights would be involved in handling Klaus's claim.
- Subrogation—The insurer would attempt to recover its claim payment for Klaus's car from Connie.
- Salvage rights—After paying Klaus, the insurer would sell what is left of Klaus's car.

3-5. It is unlikely that Sarah would comply with this request. Lisa has moved directly to negotiation and settlement without allowing Sarah to investigate the loss and provide proper valuation of the vehicle. Settling the loss in this manner would not allow Sarah to discover if there were other circumstances involved in the collision. In addition, undervaluing the vehicle would not be performing a service to Lisa.

3-6. Raymond must issue a reservation of rights letter informing the policyholder that the insurer is proceeding with the investigation of the claim but that the insurer retains its right to deny coverage later.

Educational Objective 4

4-1. The four processes involved in the claim handling for liability insurance claims are verification of coverage, determination of the cause of loss, valuation, and negotiation and settlement.

4-2. The key difference is that the claim representative must determine if the insured is legally responsible for the loss; if not, coverage does not apply.

4-3. A liability claim might result in no payment of damages under the following circumstances:
- The liability policy does not cover the loss.
- The insured under the policy is not legally responsible for the loss.

4-4. No, most liability claims are not settled by a lawsuit. Insurers often prefer to settle claims out of court because trials cost the insurer time, expense, and uncertainty.

4-5.
- $300,500—special damages
- $30,000—special damages
- $500,000—general damages
- $750,000—punitive damages

Educational Objective 5

5-1. The two primary sources of activity for insurers processing losses that originate in a catastrophe are the following:
- Processing the increased number of property claims
- Dealing with the increased scrutiny of claim handling by the media

5-2. Contingency plans before a catastrophe serve the following purposes:
- Identifying weaknesses, bottlenecks, and potential difficulties
- Permitting staff to understand their roles in advance of a crisis, so that they can react productively and not emotionally
- Permitting the organization to focus on handling claims without reallocating resources to resolve problems for which it was unprepared

5-3. It was not a good plan for Callaway's management to suspend the claim settlement authority of producers; the circumstance calls for expanded, not contracted, claim settlement authority. Likewise, it was not a good plan to add new survey and checklist forms to its claim handling procedures; it is better to develop abbreviated claim handling procedures and suspend all but critical recordkeeping. Finally, it was a good idea to authorize advance payments to policyholders who needed additional living expenses; this can help prevent negative media while helping the insureds.

Educational Objective 6

6-1. Claim representatives are required to establish loss reserves on claims that have occurred but have not yet been settled because loss reserves are liabilities that represent an estimate of the amount of claim payments the insurer will make in the future.

6-2. A case reserve is the reserve amount assigned to an individual claim.

6-3. Usually, an actuary calculates an insurer's overall loss reserves. Actuaries use case reserves as a starting point in determining overall loss reserves.

6-4. a. A loss reserve represents funds held by the insurer to pay claims for losses that have occurred but have not yet been settled. XYZ Insurance Company established a $200,000 loss reserve for James's claim as an estimate of the amount of claim payments XYZ will make in the future for this accident.

   b. Several people were injured, and the actual loss amounts may not be known for several years. The loss reserve for this accident could increase if some injuries turn out to be more severe than originally expected, and it could decrease if some claimants recover quickly. As each claim is paid, the reserve will be eliminated. When all claims are finally paid, the reserve will be removed entirely.

Educational Objective 7

7-1. One misconception a claimant may have about a claim representative is that the claim representative's job is to pay as little as possible under the insurance policy and that the only way to receive a proper recovery is through confrontational negotiation or by hiring a lawyer. A second misconception a claimant may have about a claim representative is that the claim representative represents "the other side" and is perhaps not trustworthy.

7-2. Unfair claim practices laws prohibit the following claim practices:
- Misrepresentation of material facts or insurance policy provisions relating to coverage at issue in a claim
- Failure to acknowledge and promptly respond to communications about claims arising under insurance policies
- Actions that compel an insured to sue to recover amounts due under insurance policies by offering amounts that are substantially lower than the amounts ultimately recovered in legal actions brought by such insureds
- Refusal to pay claims without first conducting a reasonable investigation based on all available information

7-3. A claim representative or an insurer may face a reprimand, fine, license suspension, substantial legal judgment, or some other legal penalty if they cannot justify claim practices that are under scrutiny.

7-4. Bill's insurer may have violated unfair claim practices laws by the following actions that are generally prohibited:
- Failure to acknowledge and promptly respond to communications with respect to claims arising under insurance policies
- Refusal to pay claims without first conducting a reasonable investigation based on all available information

SEGMENT C

Assignment 7 — Insurance Contracts

Assignment 8 — Property Loss Exposures and Policy Provisions

Assignment 9 — Liability Loss Exposures and Policy Provisions

Assignment 10 — Managing Loss Exposures: Risk Management

Segment C is the third of three segments in the INS 21 course. These segments are designed to help structure your study.

Direct Your Learning

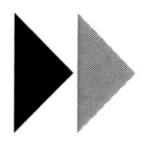

ASSIGNMENT 7

Insurance Contracts

Educational Objectives

After learning the content of this assignment, you should be able to:

1. Explain the four elements of any valid contract.
2. Describe the special characteristics of insurance contracts.
3. Describe the principle of indemnity.
4. Summarize the information usually found in the declarations page(s) of an insurance policy.
5. Explain the purpose of the following categories of insurance policy provisions:
   a. Definitions
   b. Insuring agreements
   c. Exclusions
   d. Conditions
   e. Miscellaneous provisions
6. Distinguish between manuscript policies and standard forms.
7. Describe the advantages and disadvantages of standard forms to insurers and insureds.
8. Distinguish between a self-contained policy and a modular policy.
9. Describe the conditions commonly found in property and liability insurance policies.
10. Explain how subrogation works.
11. Define or describe each of the Key Words and Phrases for this assignment.

Study Materials

Required Reading:
- Property and Liability Insurance Principles
  - Chapter 7

Study Aids:
- SMART Online Practice Exams
- SMART Study Aids
  - Review Notes and Flash Cards—Assignment 7

Outline

- **Elements of a Contract**
    - A. Agreement (Offer and Acceptance)
    - B. Competent Parties
    - C. Legal Purpose
    - D. Consideration
- **Special Characteristics of Insurance Contracts**
    - A. Conditional Contract
    - B. Contract Involving Fortuitous Events and the Exchange of Unequal Amounts
    - C. Contract of Utmost Good Faith
        1. Concealment
        2. Misrepresentation
    - D. Contract of Adhesion
    - E. Contract of Indemnity
    - F. Nontransferable Contract
- **Content of Insurance Policies**
    - A. Declarations
    - B. Definitions
    - C. Insuring Agreements
    - D. Exclusions
    - E. Conditions
    - F. Miscellaneous Provisions
- **Standard Forms and Manuscript Policies**
- **Structure of Insurance Policies**
    - A. Self-Contained Policies
    - B. Modular Policies
- **Conditions Commonly Found in Property and Liability Insurance Policies**
    - A. Cancellation
        1. Cancellation by the Insured
        2. Cancellation by the Insurer
    - B. Policy Changes
    - C. Duties of the Insured After a Loss
    - D. Assignment
    - E. Subrogation
- **Summary**

study tips: If you are not sure that you have the current materials for the exam you plan to take, please contact The Institutes.

For each assignment, you should define or describe each of the Key Words and Phrases and answer each of the Review and Application Questions.

Educational Objective 1
Explain the four essential elements of any valid contract.

Key Words and Phrases

Policy (p. 7.3)

Contract (p. 7.3)

Consideration (p. 7.5)

Review Questions

1-1. What four elements must exist for any contract to be legally enforceable? (p. 7.3)

1-2. When an insurance contract is formed: (p. 7.4)

   a. What actions generally count as an offer?

b. What actions generally count as acceptance?

1-3. What parties may not legally be competent to enter into an insurance contract? (p. 7.4)

1-4. A legally enforceable contract requires consideration by both parties to the contract. In an insurance contract: (pp. 7.5–7.6)

   a. What is the insured's consideration?

   b. What is the insurer's consideration?

Application Question

1-5. Jason found a Web site on the Internet that offered quotations and online applications for automobile insurance. Jason entered the appropriate information and approved the quotation of the premium. The Internet Web site then confirmed that Jason qualified for coverage and presented an application for him to complete. Jason completed the online application, entered his credit card number for payment of the premium, and clicked "submit application." He then jumped into his car feeling confident that he had coverage in case he had an accident. Explain whether Jason's transactions fulfilled the four essential elements of a contract between Jason and the Internet insurer. (pp. 7.4–7.6)

Educational Objective 2

Describe the special characteristics of insurance contracts.

Key Words and Phrases

Conditional contract (p. 7.6)

Utmost good faith (p. 7.7)

Concealment (p. 7.8)

Material fact (p. 7.8)

Misrepresentation (p. 7.8)

Contract of adhesion (p. 7.9)

Review Questions

2-1. List the six distinct characteristics of an insurance policy. (p. 7.6)

2-2. Insurance is considered a conditional contract because one or more parties must perform only under certain conditions. XYZ Insurance Company has issued an auto insurance policy to Bill Jones. (p. 7.6)

 a. What conditions may occur that obligate XYZ to perform some duties to fulfill its obligations to Bill?

 b. If the conditions in your answer to a. above do not occur, has Bill's insurance been worthless? Explain.

2-3. Insurance buyers agree to pay a premium, and insurers agree to pay claims. Why does this contract involve an exchange of unequal amounts? (pp. 7.6–7.7)

2-4. Why is insurance considered a contract of utmost good faith? (p. 7.7)

2-5. What is the distinction between *concealment* and *misrepresentation*? (p. 7.8)

Application Question

2-6. An insured who has recently been involved in a minor auto accident states: "I have been driving for fifteen years and never had an auto accident. Now I finally have a chance to get back those thousands of dollars of premiums I have paid over the years, so I am going to take the insurer for everything I can get." Explain why this person has a misconception concerning how insurance policies are designed to work. (pp. 7.6–7.7)

Educational Objective 3

Describe the principle of indemnity.

Key Words and Phrases

Contract of indemnity (p. 7.9)

Principle of indemnity (p. 7.10)

Valued policy (p. 7.10)

Review Questions

3-1. Explain how the following types of insurance act as contracts of indemnity: (pp. 7.9–7.10)

    a. Property insurance

    b. Liability insurance

3-2. Identify two factors enforcing the principle of indemnity. (p. 7.10)

3-3. A liability insurance policy promises to pay any covered claims against the insured up to a limit of $100,000. Is this a valued policy or a contract of indemnity? Explain. (pp. 7.9–7.10)

Application Question

3-4. A fire in Evelyn's apartment burned her five-year-old sofa. Evelyn received a check from her insurer for $1,000, which was the cost of a new sofa ($1,500) minus the depreciation on the sofa because it was five years old ($300) and minus her deductible ($200). Evelyn was angry because she had a nice sofa and was not able to replace it with the $1,000 that she received. Explain whether the principle of indemnity has been satisfied in this transaction. (p. 7.10)

Educational Objective 4

Summarize the information usually found on the declarations page(s) of an insurance policy.

Key Word or Phrase

Declarations page, or declarations, or dec. (p. 7.11)

Review Questions

4-1. What kinds of information are found in the declarations of a typical insurance policy? (p. 7.12)

4-2. Provide an example in which an insurer might pay an amount greater than the policy limit on a liability policy. (p. 7.12)

4-3. Provide an example in which an insurer might pay an amount greater than the policy limit on a property policy. (p. 7.12)

Application Question

4-4. Ralph is a new customer service representative at an insurer. He received a call from a policyholder who had just experienced an accident but had not been able to collect the names and phone numbers of the witnesses. She wanted to have that information available when she submitted the claim. The policyholder asked Ralph how quickly she was required to submit the claim. Ralph opened her file and began reviewing the policyholder's declarations page to determine an answer. Explain whether Ralph will locate the answer on the declarations page. (pp. 7.12, 7.24)

Educational Objective 5

Explain the purpose of the following categories of insurance policy provisions:

a. Definitions
b. Insuring agreements
c. Exclusions
d. Conditions
e. Miscellaneous provisions

Key Words and Phrases

Insuring agreement (p. 7.16)

Exclusion (p. 7.16)

Policy condition (p. 7.17)

Review Questions

5-1. Why do many insurance policies include definitions of the terms used in the policy? (p. 7.12)

5-2. An insurance pundit stated, "The large print giveth but the fine print taketh away." How does this tongue-in-cheek statement explain the relationship between an insurance policy's insuring agreement and its exclusions? (p. 7.16)

5-3. What are eight major reasons why insurance policies contain exclusions? (pp. 7.16–7.17)

Application Question

5-4. Angelica is a telecommuter who uses her computer to complete her work and correspond with her employer. Her computer was damaged in a lightning storm, and she is trying to determine whether the damage is covered by her homeowners insurance policy. What sections of the policy should Angelica review to determine whether her loss is covered? (pp. 7.12–7.18)

Educational Objective 6

Distinguish between manuscript policies and standard forms.

Key Word or Phrase

Manuscript policy, or manuscript endorsement (p. 7.18)

Review Question

6-1. Distinguish between a manuscript policy and a standard form. (p. 7.18)

Educational Objective 7

Describe the advantages and disadvantages of standard forms to insurers and insureds.

Review Questions

7-1. What are the advantages of standard insurance policies and forms for the following? (p. 7.19)

   a. Insurers

   b. Insureds

c. Anyone interpreting insurance policies

7-2. Explain why insurers are at an advantage when standardized wording is used in insurance policies of the same type. (p. 7.19)

Application Question

7-3. A colonial museum owns and displays the field tent that George Washington used during the Revolutionary War. The tent is often loaned to other museums for display. The museum would like to insure the tent from damage or destruction and has approached the XYZ Insurance Company to write that coverage. Would the XYZ Insurance Company be more likely to use a manuscript or a standard form policy to write this coverage? (pp. 7.18–7.19)

Educational Objective 8
Distinguish between a self-contained policy and a modular policy.

Key Words and Phrases

Self-contained policy (p. 7.19)

Endorsement (p. 7.20)

Modular policy (p. 7.20)

Review Questions

8-1. Both self-contained and modular insurance policies include declarations, insuring agreements, conditions, and exclusions. How do these two types of policies differ? (pp. 7.19–7.20)

8-2. Explain how an endorsement might modify a personal auto policy to conform to the requirements of the state in which the insured lives. (p. 7.20)

8-3. Identify the two mandatory components of an ISO commercial package policy (CPP) and describe what each component contains. (p. 7.20)

Application Question

8-4. XYZ Insurance Company is developing a new policy for individuals living in retirement communities. The policy is flexible in that it can include coverage for a home that an insured owns or just the contents of a living unit owned by the retirement community. The policy can also include liability coverage, golf cart coverage, coverage for jewelry and furs, personal automobile coverage, travel insurance, and limited coverage for devices such as hearing aids, glasses, and dentures. Would you recommend that XYZ establish this coverage in a self-contained policy or in a modular policy? (pp. 7.19–7.20)

Educational Objective 9
Describe the conditions commonly found in property and liability insurance policies.

Key Words and Phrases
Cancellation (p. 7.23)

Pro rata refund (p. 7.23)

Short rate refund (p. 7.23)

Liberalization clause (p. 7.24)

Assignment (p. 7.24)

Review Questions

9-1. Briefly explain the information that appears under each of the following headings in a typical insurance policy. (pp. 7.23–7.25)

    a. Cancellation

    b. Policy changes

    c. Duties of the insured after a loss

    d. Assignment

9-2. Explain how an insured's premium would be affected in each of the following situations: (p. 7.23)

   a. The insurer cancels the insurance policy

   b. The insured cancels the insurance policy

9-3. Describe an insured's duties after a loss involving the following types of insurance policies: (p. 7.24)

   a. Property insurance policies

   b. Liability insurance policies

Application Question

9-4. Ralph, a customer service representative of an insurer, has received a telephone call from a policyholder who has sold her home. She would like to know what she must do to cancel her homeowners policy and what refund she will receive. Will Ralph be able to answer the policyholder's questions by referring to the conditions section of her homeowners policy? (p. 7.23)

Educational Objective 10
Explain how subrogation works.

Review Questions

10-1. Explain the effect of subrogation on the insured's right of recovery. (pp. 7.25–7.26)

10-2. Provide an example in which an insurance policy would permit an insured to waive rights of recovery before a loss. (p. 7.26)

Application Question

10-3. Jerry is a contractor working in Sue's building. Through Jerry's negligence a fire starts, causing damage to Sue's building. After the fire, Sue feels sorry for Jerry and says, "You don't need to pay for my building damage—I'm fully insured." (pp. 7.25–7.26)

   a. In investigating the loss, Sue's property insurer discovers that Sue has released Jerry from liability. Cite the specific policy provision(s) that would explain why that discovery is likely to affect the insurer's payment of Sue's claim.

   b. If Sue had released Jerry from liability for fire damage to the building before the loss occurred, would that have affected Sue's coverage for a subsequent loss caused by Jerry's negligence? Explain.

Answers to Assignment 7 Questions

NOTE: These answers are provided to give students a basic understanding of acceptable types of responses. They often are not the only valid answers and are not intended to provide an exhaustive response to the questions.

Educational Objective 1

1-1. Four elements that must exist for a contract to be legally enforceable include the following:
- Agreement (offer and acceptance)
- Competent parties
- Legal purpose
- Consideration

1-2. a. When an insurance contract is formed, the action that counts as an offer is when someone who wants to purchase insurance completes an insurance application.

b. When an insurance contract is formed, the action that counts as an acceptance is when an insurer underwriter (or an agent, acting on behalf of an insurer) accepts the application and agrees to provide the coverage requested at a price acceptable to both the insurer and the applicant.

1-3. Parties that may not legally be competent to enter into an insurance contract include the following:
- Insane or otherwise mentally incompetent parties
- Parties under the influence of drugs or alcohol
- Minors (persons not yet of legal age)

1-4. a. In an insurance contract, the insured's consideration is payment of the premium or the promise to pay.

b. In an insurance contract, the insurer's consideration is the promise to pay claims for covered losses.

1-5. Presuming that Jason is a competent party, it appears that a contract has been completed between Jason and the Internet insurer.
- There seems to have been an offer and acceptance. The offer occurred when Jason entered the appropriate information and approved the quotation of the premium. The insurer's acceptance was its confirmation that Jason qualified for coverage. There was mutual assent at that point.
- Insurance for an automobile is a legal purpose.
- Jason submitted his payment, which would be the consideration for the contract.

Educational Objective 2

2-1. An insurance policy is: a conditional contract, a contract involving fortuitous events and the exchange of unequal amounts, a contract of the utmost good faith, a contract of adhesion, a contract of indemnity, and a nontransferable contract.

2-2. a. Conditions that may obligate an insurer to perform duties to fulfill its obligations to an insured include the following:
- Occurrence of a covered loss
- Prompt notification of a loss by the insured

b. No, Bill's insurance has not been worthless. The promise of the insurer to make payments if a covered loss occurs exists, even if the insurer's performance is not required during the policy period.

2-3. The insurance contract involves an exchange of unequal amounts (an insured pays premiums and an insurer pays claims) because sometimes only a small loss or no loss occurs during the policy period, and the premium paid by the insured is more than the amount paid by the insurer. Other times, a large loss may occur, and the insurer's claim payment may be much more than the premium paid by the insured.

2-4. Insurance is considered a contract of utmost good faith because insurance involves a promise that requires complete honesty and disclosure of all relevant facts from both parties. Both parties to an insurance contract are expected to be ethical in their dealings with one another.

2-5. The distinction between concealment and misrepresentation is that concealment is an intentional failure to disclose a material fact (omission) but a misrepresentation is a false statement of a material fact (falsehood).

2-6. This insured does not understand that an auto policy is designed to work as a conditional contract and as a contract involving the exchange of unequal amounts.
- The insurer must perform only under certain conditions, such as when a covered loss occurs during the policy period.
- The premium paid by the insured for a particular policy can be, and often is, more than the amount paid by the insurer to, or on behalf of, the insured for a covered loss.

Educational Objective 3

3-1. a. As a contract of indemnity, property insurance generally pays the amount necessary to repair covered property that has been damaged or to replace it with similar property.

b. As a contract of indemnity, liability insurance generally pays to a third-party claimant, on behalf of the insured, any amounts (up to the policy limit) that the insured becomes legally obligated to pay as damages for a covered liability claim, as well as the legal costs associated with that claim.

3-2. One factor that enforces the principle of indemnity is that insurance policies generally contain an "other insurance" provision to prevent an insured from receiving full payment from two different insurance policies for the same claim. A second factor that enforces the principle of indemnity is that a person cannot buy insurance unless that person is in a position to suffer a financial loss.

3-3. A liability insurance policy that promises to pay any covered claims against the insured up to a limit of $100,000 is a contract of indemnity because the insurer agrees to pay an amount directly related to the amount of the loss up to the limit. A valued policy would pay a stated amount (such as $100,000) regardless of the actual amount of the loss.

3-4. Yes, the principle of indemnity has been satisfied. The principle of indemnity states that the insured should not be better off financially after a loss than before. Evelyn did not have a new sofa. She had a sofa that she used and enjoyed for five years. She was given the cost of a new sofa minus the use of that item. The $200 deductible is a condition of the policy and is not a factor in the principle of indemnity.

Educational Objective 4

4-1. The declarations of a typical insurance policy contain the following information:
- Name and location of the insurer
- Name and address of the insured
- Policy number
- Policy period (inception and expiration dates)
- Description of covered property or locations
- Coverage limits
- Deductibles
- Premium(s)
- Policy forms
- List of endorsements, if any

4-2. Defense costs are an example of when an insurer may pay an amount greater than the policy limit on a liability policy.

4-3. Additional coverages, such as debris removal, are an example of when an insurer may pay an amount greater than the policy limit on a property policy.

4-4. No, the time requirement for submitting claims is not contained on the declarations page. The information is located in the conditions section of the policy.

Educational Objective 5

5-1. Insurance policies include definitions of the terms used in the policy because insurance often contains technical terms or words that are used in a very specific way.

5-2. An insurance policy's insuring agreement "giveth" by stating that the insurer will make a payment or provide a service, under certain circumstances. The exclusions "taketh away" by eliminating coverage for specified exposures.

5-3. Eight major reasons why insurance policies contain exclusions are as follows:
- To eliminate duplicate coverage
- To assist in managing moral hazards
- To avoid insuring other losses that are deliberate
- To assist in managing attitudinal (morale) hazards
- To avoid covering losses that are not economically feasible to insure
- To eliminate coverage that most insureds do not need
- To eliminate coverage for exposures that require special handling by the insurer
- To keep premiums reasonable

5-4. Angelica should review the following policy sections:
- The definitions will describe any technical terms or words that are used in the policy.
- The insuring agreement will describe the broad circumstances under which payment or service is provided by the insurer.
- The exclusions will help Angelica determine whether the computer used for business is excluded from coverage or if the peril of lightning is excluded.
- The conditions will help Angelica determine what information she must gather for the claim and how quickly the claim must be submitted.

Educational Objective 6

6-1. A manuscript policy and a standard form differ in that a manuscript policy's terms are negotiated and drafted only in a special situation for a specific purpose, usually involving a large amount of insurance. A standard form contains standardized policy wording and is used for any insured accepted for a particular coverage.

Educational Objective 7

7-1. a. The advantages to insurers of standard insurance policies and forms are as follows:
- Efficiency in providing insurance
- Less time and expense in issuing the policy
- Consistency in underwriting and claim handling
- Underwriting and pricing based on the court's predictable interpretations

b. The advantages to insureds of standard insurance policies and forms are as follows:
- No need to compare differences in policy provisions and language
- Fewer claim disputes if the loss is covered by several insurers

c. The advantages to others of standard insurance policies and forms are as follows:
- A more consistent and predictable interpretation of insurance policies
- Less possibility of a disputed interpretation because terms and clauses used elsewhere in the same policy or in different policies are often repeated

7-2. Insurers are at an advantage when standardized wording is used in insurance policies of the same type because they know how the court is likely to interpret this language in the future and can properly underwrite and price the policy based on that interpretation.

7-3. One could argue that, although the tent is a unique item, the loss exposures to the tent are not unique: theft, vandalism, fire, and so forth. By that logic, it is likely that XYZ would use a standard form to provide coverage. The standard form provides the advantage of common language and provisions that can reduce the likelihood of a claim dispute and provide a more consistent interpretation of insurance policies. Alternatively, one could argue that the tent owners desire more than the replacement cost value for the tent, given its historic importance, and therefore a manuscript policy may be required.

Educational Objective 8

8-1. A self-contained policy is a single document containing all the agreements between the insurer and the insured and forming a complete policy by itself. A modular policy consists of several different documents, none of which by itself forms a complete contract.

8-2. An endorsement may modify a personal auto policy to conform to the requirements of the state in which the insured lives by placing some state-specific restrictions on the insurer's cancellation provision.

8-3. The two mandatory components of an ISO commercial package policy (CPP) are the common policy declarations and the common policy conditions. The common policy declarations contain information that applies to the entire policy, such as the insured's name and address, the policy period, and the coverage(s) for which a premium has been or will be paid. The common policy conditions are standard provisions that apply to all CPPs, regardless of the coverages included.

8-4. Because so many different coverages can be included in the same policy, it could be beneficial for XYZ to establish this as a modular policy. Then only those components of coverage required can be attached to the policy. (Answers may vary.)

Educational Objective 9

9-1. a. In a typical insurance policy, cancellation can be made at any time with written notice by the insured or by the insurer for certain reasons. The insurer must provide advance written notice of cancellation to the insured and must pay any return premium to the named insured.

b. In a typical insurance policy, the policy can be changed only by a written endorsement issued by the insurer.

c. In a typical insurance policy, the duties of the insured after a loss are to notify the insurer "promptly" or "as soon as practical," cooperate with the insurer, and perform certain other duties which vary depending on the coverage.

d. In a typical insurance policy, the insured is not permitted to transfer its rights and duties under the policy without written consent of the insurer.

9-2. a. If the insurer cancels the insurance policy, the insured is entitled to a refund of the premium, on a pro rata basis.

b. If the insured cancels the insurance policy, the premium refund may be less than pro rata. This cancellation penalty (also known as short rate charge) reflects the fact that the insurer incurred some expense in issuing the policy.

9-3. a. Property insurance policies generally require the insured to prepare an inventory of damaged and undamaged property and to protect the property from further damage.

b. Liability insurance policies usually require the insured to promptly forward all papers regarding a claim or suit to the insurer. Other specific duties of the insured are determined by the type of coverage provided and by the policy wording.

9-4. Yes, the conditions section of the policy specifies what the policyholder must do to cancel the policy. The conditions section also provides information about the refund that will be due to the policyholder.

Educational Objective 10

10-1. The effect of subrogation on the insured's right of recovery is that the insured would transfer its rights of recovery against others to the insurer for losses the insurer has paid to an insured. When an insurer pays an insured for a loss, the insurer takes over the insured's right to collect damages from a third party responsible for the loss.

10-2. An insurance policy would permit an insured to waive rights of recovery before a loss in the case of a property lease that states the tenant will not be held responsible for accidental damage to property owned by the insured. The insurer will have no right to recover from the tenant if the tenant accidentally causes a fire that damages the insured's property.

10-3. a. Sue's insurer may decline to pay for Sue's loss because she has violated her policy's subrogation provision. This provision obligates Sue to do nothing after a loss to impair the insurer's rights of recovery against a responsible party—in this case, the negligent contractor. By waiving her rights against Jerry, Sue may prevent her insurer from taking over those rights by subrogation.

b. No. If Sue had waived her rights against Jerry before the loss occurred (perhaps in the contract she signed to obtain Jerry's services), Sue's insurer would not withhold payment for a fire loss caused by Jerry. The subrogation provision often allows the insured to waive recovery rights before a loss.

Direct Your Learning

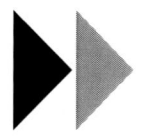

Assignment 8

Property Loss Exposures and Policy Provisions

Educational Objectives

After learning the content of this assignment, you should be able to:

1. Describe the types of property that may be exposed to loss and that are typically covered by property insurance.
2. Explain how causes of loss (perils) are treated in named perils policies and in special form policies, and their effect on burden of proof.
3. Describe the financial consequences of property losses.
4. Explain how parties with an insurable interest would be affected by property losses.
5. Describe the types of property and their locations commonly covered in property insurance policies.
6. Explain how property insurance policies typically describe covered causes of loss.
7. Explain why property insurance policies usually exclude some causes of loss.
8. Describe the financial consequences of loss that may be covered by property insurance policies.
9. Identify the parties that can be covered by property insurance policies.
10. Explain how property insurance policies provide coverage for the named insured and other parties.
11. Explain how policy limits and other provisions affect the amount of recovery under a property insurance policy.
12. Define or describe each of the Key Words and Phrases for this assignment.

Study Materials

Required Reading:
- Property and Liability Insurance Principles
  - Chapter 8

Study Aids:
- SMART Online Practice Exams
- SMART Study Aids
  - Review Notes and Flash Cards—Assignment 8

Outline

- **Property Loss Exposures**
    - A. Types of Property
        1. Buildings
        2. Personal Property (Contents) Contained in Buildings
        3. Money and Securities
        4. Motor Vehicles and Trailers
        5. Property in Transit
        6. Ships and Their Cargoes
        7. Boilers and Machinery
    - B. Causes of Loss to Property
        1. Perils and Hazards
        2. Burden of Proof
    - C. Financial Consequences of Property Losses
        1. Reduced Property Value
        2. Lost Income
        3. Extra Expenses
    - D. Parties Affected by Property Losses
        1. Property Owners
        2. Secured Lenders
        3. Property Users
        4. Property Holders
- **Property Insurance Policy Provisions**
    - A. Covered Property and Locations
        1. Dwellings, Buildings, and Other Structures
        2. Personal Property
        3. Property Other Than the Insured's Buildings and Contents
    - B. Covered Causes of Loss
        1. Basic Form Coverage
        2. Broad Form Coverage
        3. Special Form (Open Perils) Coverage
        4. Collapse
        5. Crime Perils
        6. Auto Physical Damage
    - C. Causes of Loss Often Excluded
        1. Catastrophe Perils
        2. Maintenance Perils
    - D. Covered Financial Consequences
        1. Reduction in Property Value (Direct Loss)
        2. Time Element (Indirect) Loss
    - E. Covered Parties
        1. Named Insured(s)
        2. Secured Lenders
        3. Other Parties Whose Property Is Covered
    - F. Amounts of Recovery
        1. Policy Limits
        2. Valuation Provisions
        3. Settlement Options
        4. Deductibles
        5. Insurance-to-Value Provisions
        6. "Other Insurance" Provisions
- **Summary**

Reward yourself after you reach specific goals.

For each assignment, you should define or describe each of the Key Words and Phrases and answer each of the Review and Application Questions.

> ## Educational Objective 1
> Describe the types of property that may be exposed to loss and that are typically covered by property insurance.

Key Words and Phrases

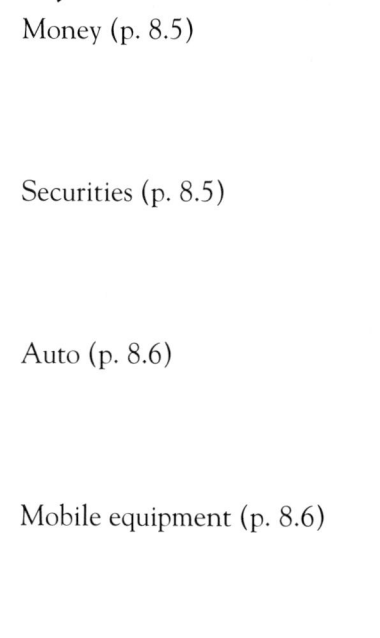

Money (p. 8.5)

Securities (p. 8.5)

Auto (p. 8.6)

Mobile equipment (p. 8.6)

Recreational vehicle (p. 8.6)

Review Questions

1-1. What types of property may be exposed to loss by an insurable cause of loss (peril) that results in adverse financial consequences? (pp. 8.4–8.7)

1-2. Why do property insurance policies refer to "personal property" rather than "contents"? (p. 8.5)

Application Question

1-3. A household products company owns a large factory in which it manufactures consumer products. Identify three types of property, other than its building, that may be covered by the household products company's property insurance. (p. 8.4)

Educational Objective 2

Explain how causes of loss (perils) are treated in named perils policies and in special form policies, and their effect on burden of proof.

Key Words and Phrases

Cause of loss, or peril (p. 8.7)

Named peril (p. 8.7)

Special form, or open perils policy (p. 8.7)

Review Questions

2-1. In addition to altering the property itself, what other effect can a cause of loss have? (p. 8.7)

2-2. Identify an important difference between named perils and special form (open perils) coverage. (p. 8.8)

2-3. From the point of view of the insured, why is it an advantage to shift the burden of proof to the insurer by purchasing open perils (special form) coverage? (p. 8.8)

Application Question

2-4. A friend, Brian, has called you to ask for advice in purchasing insurance for a home he is buying. He has a choice of purchasing coverage on a named perils basis or on a special form coverage policy. He is using most of his financial assets to purchase the home, so he wants to make sure that as many significant losses as possible will be covered. Recommend coverage for Brian and justify your response. (p. 8.7)

Educational Objective 3

Describe the financial consequences of property losses.

Review Questions

3-1. Give an example of each of the following potential financial consequences to the owner of a grocery store that burns. (pp. 8.8–8.10)

    a. Reduction in value of property

    b. Lost income

    c. Increased expenses

3-2. Explain why items such as fine paintings or other art objects are worth less after they are repaired than they would have been if they had never been damaged. (p. 8.9)

Application Question

3-3. A bakery purchased a custom-made croissant machine from a French manufacturer that has no service representative or parts outlet in the United States. If the bakery's croissant machine is damaged in a fire, one financial consequence will be a decrease in the value of the machine. Explain another financial consequence that would be likely to result from damage to the machine. (pp. 8.9–8.10)

Educational Objective 4

Explain how parties with an insurable interest would be affected by property losses.

Key Words and Phrases

Mortgagee, or mortgageholder (p. 8.11)

Mortgagor (p. 8.11)

Bailee (p. 8.11)

Review Questions

4-1. Who besides the property owner is likely to be affected by a property loss? Explain. (pp. 8.10–8.11)

4-2. Explain how property insurance policies protect the secured lender's interest in the financed property. (p. 8.11)

Application Question

4-3. With the aid of a mortgage from his bank, Alfred purchased a building containing five apartments. All of the apartments are rented to tenants. Briefly explain why (a) the bank and (b) the tenants may have a financial loss if Alfred's building is destroyed by a fire. (p. 8.11)

Educational Objective 5
Describe the types of property and their locations commonly covered in property insurance policies.

Key Words and Phrases
Property insurance (p. 8.11)

Floater (p. 8.12)

Review Questions

5-1. Describe two challenges faced by insurers when stating the location of covered property in a building. (p. 8.12)

5-2. Identify at least one item of property of each of the following types that can be covered by an insurance policy. If possible, list an item that is not entirely obvious. For example, it is not obvious that an insurance policy may define "buildings" to include lawn mowers used to service the surrounding land. (pp. 8.13–8.15)

   a. Buildings

   b. Personal property

   c. Property other than the insured's buildings and contents

5-3. Why is it important to specify whether a garage is part of the dwelling or qualifies as an other structure? (p. 8.13)

Application Question

5-4. Kim owns a dwelling that she has just renovated to be occupied by a tenant. The dwelling will be rented without furniture, so Kim has purchased a policy to cover only the structure and no personal property contents. One significant expense in the renovation was the $10,000 wall-to-wall carpet that Kim installed throughout the house. How would you recommend that Kim determine whether the carpet is covered as part of the dwelling or should be added as personal property contents? (pp. 8.13–8.14)

Educational Objective 6
Explain how property insurance policies typically describe covered causes of loss.

Key Words and Phrases

Friendly fire (p. 8.16)

Hostile fire (p. 8.16)

Proximate cause (p. 8.17)

Vehicle damage (p. 8.18)

Vandalism (p. 8.19)

Sprinkler leakage (p. 8.19)

Sinkhole collapse (p. 8.20)

Mine subsidence (p. 8.20)

Volcanic action (p. 8.20)

Burglary (p. 8.21)

Robbery (p. 8.22)

Theft (p. 8.22)

Collision (p. 8.22)

Other than collision, or comprehensive (p. 8.22)

Specified causes of loss (p. 8.22)

Review Questions

6-1. Explain the key differences between basic, broad, and special form (open perils) property insurance coverage. (p. 8.16)

6-2. What perils are typically covered under a property insurance policy that covers the basic causes of loss? (p. 8.16)

6-3. What additional perils are covered by a broad form property insurance policy? (p. 8.21)

6-4. Both burglary and robbery are examples of theft. What is the distinction between burglary and robbery? (pp. 8.21–8.22)

Application Question

6-5. Placido and Maria have just purchased their first home and they are shopping for homeowners insurance. With the help of an insurance agent, they examined the exclusions of the basic, broad, and special form coverage policies. They found that none of those policies specifically excluded some types of coverage that they wanted in regards to accidents caused by occupants of a dwelling. For example, they want to be covered in the event that they place a hot pan on the counter and scorch the surface or accidentally spill bleach on a hardwood floor and ruin the surface. Which of those policy forms will meet their coverage needs? (pp. 8.16–8.22)

Educational Objective 7
Explain why property insurance policies usually exclude some causes of loss.

Review Questions

7-1. Identify the two perils that are often excluded in property insurance policies. (pp. 8.22–8.23)

7-2. Provide some examples of the two perils identified in your answer to Question 7-1. (p. 8.23)

7-3. For each of the perils identified in your answer to Question 7-1, explain why each is excluded from property insurance policies. (pp. 8.22–8.23)

Application Question

7-4. Some policyholders seek coverage for every loss that occurs. However, insurance policies exclude coverage for many maintenance perils. Do you think that the coverage of maintenance perils by insurance policies would lead to attitudinal hazards? (p. 8.23)

Educational Objective 8
Describe the financial consequences of loss that may be covered by property insurance policies.

Key Words and Phrases
Direct loss (p. 8.24)

Time element loss, or indirect loss (p. 8.24)

Extra expenses (p. 8.24)

Additional living expense (p. 8.25)

Review Questions

8-1. Give an example of a time element loss. (p. 8.24)

8-2. Regarding business income insurance, briefly describe the two items included in covered business income. (p. 8.24)

8-3. Identify extra expenses that would be covered for an insurance agent who wishes to conduct business at a temporary location during the repairs to his or her office building following a fire. (p. 8.24)

Application Question

8-4. Consider your own home or apartment. If a loss damaged your home and required two months to repair, what financial consequences would you experience as a result that might be covered by the additional living expense coverage of your homeowners, tenant homeowners, or dwelling policy? (p. 8.25)

Educational Objective 9

Identify the parties that can be covered by property insurance policies.

Review Question

9-1. Identify persons or organizations with an insurable interest in property and describe how property insurance policies are written to cover these various interests. (p. 8.25)

Educational Objective 10

Explain how property insurance policies provide coverage for the named insured and other parties.

Key Words and Phrases

Named insured (p. 8.25)

First named insured (p. 8.26)

Mortgage clause, or mortgageholders clause (p. 8.26)

Loss payee (p. 8.27)

Loss payable clause (p. 8.27)

Review Questions

10-1. What rights does the mortgage clause in an insurance policy give to a mortgagee (mortgageholder) who is named in the declarations of that insurance policy? (pp. 8.26–8.27)

10-2. Provide two examples of coverage provided by a homeowners policy to parties who are neither named insureds nor secured lenders. (p. 8.27)

Application Question

10-3. Pradeep is a tenant in an apartment building. Pradeep uses a wheelchair and has installed fixtures in the apartment that help him in the use of the bathroom and kitchen. Explain whether Pradeep has an insurable interest in the fixtures and how he might obtain insurance coverage for them. (p. 8.25)

Educational Objective 11

Explain how policy limits and other provisions affect the amount of recovery under a property insurance policy.

Key Words and Phrases

Deductible (p. 8.29)

Insurance-to-value provision (p. 8.29)

Coinsurance (p. 8.30)

Review Questions

11-1. Why do insurance policies contain deductibles? (p. 8.29)

11-2. Atley Corporation owns an office building that is insured under a property insurance policy issued by Radley Insurance Company. A fire caused extensive damage to Atley's building. Explain how each of the following may affect the amount paid by Radley Insurance Company to repair the fire damage to Atley's building. (pp. 8.28–8.30)

  a. Policy limits

b. Deductible provision

c. Insurance-to-value provision

d. "Other insurance" provision

Application Question

11-3. Why do insurance policies contain provisions designed to encourage insurance to value? (pp. 8.29–8.30)

Answers to Assignment 8 Questions

NOTE: These answers are provided to give students a basic understanding of acceptable types of responses. They often are not the only valid answers and are not intended to provide an exhaustive response to the questions.

Educational Objective 1

1-1. The following types of property might be exposed to loss by an insurable cause of loss (peril) that results in adverse financial consequences:
- Buildings—building materials, plumbing, wiring, heating and air conditioning equipment, and portable equipment to service the building and surrounding land
- Personal property contained in buildings—furniture and fixtures, machinery and equipment, and stock (contents)
- Money and securities—currency, coins, bank notes, traveler's checks, credit card slips, money orders held for sale to the public, and written instruments representing either money or property
- Motor vehicles and trailers—autos and other highway vehicles, mobile equipment, and recreational vehicles
- Property in transit—cargo
- Ships and their cargoes
- Boilers and machinery

1-2. Property insurance policies refer to "personal property" rather than "contents" because the property is often covered even when it is not literally contained in the building. (Note: When the contents of a commercial building are involved, policies generally use the term "business personal property.")

1-3. Property that may be covered by the household products company's property insurance includes the following:
- Furniture and fixtures—chairs, tables, shelving, and lighting
- Machinery—manufacturing equipment
- Stock—completed products and manufacturing supplies

Educational Objective 2

2-1. In addition to altering the property itself, a cause of loss can result in a person's inability to use the property—for example, when property is stolen.

2-2. An important difference between named perils and special form (open perils) coverage involves the burden of proof. For named perils, the burden of proof is on the insured; for special form (open perils) coverage, the burden of proof is on the insurer.

2-3. From an insured's point of view it is advantageous to shift the burden of proof to the insurer by purchasing open perils coverage because if an insured has a property loss, coverage applies unless the insurer can prove that an excluded peril caused the loss.

2-4. Special form coverage will provide protection for more perils than will a named perils policy. The special form coverage provides protection for any direct loss unless the loss is caused by an excluded peril. This method of providing coverage is broader than named perils, which covers only those perils specifically named in the policy.

Educational Objective 3

3-1. The owner of a grocery store can have the following financial consequences from a major fire:
   a. A reduction in value of property can result from property damage—The building and property within (freezers and shelves) may have to be repaired or replaced. Smoke-damaged stock will have to be replaced.
   b. Lost income can result from a business interruption—Retail sales will not be made while the store is closed for repairs (restoration period).
   c. Increased expenses can result because the building owner may need to rent another building to conduct its business while the original building is being repaired.

3-2. Items such as fine paintings or other art objects are worth less than they would be if they had never been damaged because their value depends on their being in mint or original condition. An object that has been repaired after damage from a tear, scratch, or fire is no longer in that unspoiled condition, and its value will decline.

3-3. Another financial consequence of a loss to a foreign custom-made machine would probably be lost income. Without the machine, the bakery would be unable to make its croissants until the machine is replaced or repaired and would probably lose income from lost sales.

Educational Objective 4

4-1. Besides the property owner, the following individuals may be affected by a property loss:
   - Secured lenders of money to the property owner have conditional rights to that property. If the property is damaged or destroyed, the secured lenders will lose their rights (such as repossession of property).
   - Users of the property may have signed a rental lease specifying a low rental rate. If the building is destroyed, the lease will be canceled, and the user may have to pay a higher rent elsewhere.
   - Other holders of the property are responsible for property entrusted to them by others. If the property is destroyed, the holder of the property (bailee) is liable for that property.

4-2. Property insurance policies protect the secured lender's interest in the financed property by naming the lender on the insurance policy and by giving the lender certain rights under the policy.

4-3. a. The bank has an insurable interest in the apartment building until the mortgage is paid in full because the borrower pledged the apartment as security for the mortgage loan. Destruction of the apartment building would reduce the value of the property and cause the bank a financial loss in the event of a mortgage default.
   b. Destruction of the property could cause cancellation of the tenants' leases and result in financial loss. For example, a tenant may have a lease at a rental rate much lower than the current rental value of comparable premises and may be unable to obtain as favorable a lease upon cancellation. Another tenant may have paid advance rent that is not recoverable under the terms of the lease.

Educational Objective 5

5-1. One challenge faced by insurers when stating the location of covered property lies in describing precisely what is and is not covered under an insurance policy that provides building coverage. Another challenge lies in the fact that buildings and personal property do not necessarily remain at a fixed location. For example, window screens may be removed from the building and placed in storage during the winter while storm windows are being used.

5-2. Examples of property that can be covered by an insurance policy are as follows:
   a. Building property—wall-to-wall carpeting
   b. Personal property—valuable papers
   c. Property other than building or contents—an automobile

5-3. It is important to specify whether a garage is part of the dwelling or qualifies as an other structure because different policy limits (dollar amounts of insurance) apply for the dwelling and for other structures.

5-4. Kim should check the definition of "residence premises" included in the dwelling policy. It will define items that are considered part of the residence and those that are specifically excluded from coverage.

Educational Objective 6

6-1. The key differences between basic, broad, and special form (open perils) property insurance coverage include the following:
   - Basic form coverage provides the lowest-cost coverage for approximately a dozen named perils.
   - Broad form coverage provides a higher-cost coverage that adds several perils to those in the basic coverage.
   - Special form (open perils) coverage provides coverage for all causes of loss that are not specifically excluded. (Special form coverage adds to the perils included in broad form coverage.)

6-2. Perils typically covered under a property insurance policy that covers the basic causes of loss include the following:
   - Fire and lightning
   - Windstorm
   - Hail
   - Aircraft
   - Vehicle damage
   - Riot and civil commotion
   - Explosion
   - Smoke
   - Vandalism
   - Sprinkler leakage
   - Sinkhole collapse
   - Volcanic action

6-3. Additional perils covered by a broad form property insurance policy include the following:
   - Falling objects
   - Weight of snow, ice, or sleet
   - Sudden and accidental water damage

6-4. Burglary is theft by someone who breaks into a building and illegally removes property; robbery is theft committed by someone who takes property from a person in the presence of that person using intimidation or force.

6-5. Only the special form policy will provide the needed coverage. The special form covers all perils not specifically excluded. Even though the basic and broad forms do not specifically exclude these perils, each covers listed perils only.

Educational Objective 7

7-1. Two perils that are often excluded in property insurance policies are catastrophe perils and maintenance perils.

7-2. Some examples of catastrophe perils include war, nuclear hazard, flood, and earthquake. Some examples of maintenance perils include wear and tear; marring and scratching; rust; gradual seepage of water; and damage by insects, birds, rodents, or other animals.

7-3. Catastrophe perils are excluded from property insurance policies because they affect many people at the same time with such widespread losses that the funds of the entire insurance business might be inadequate to pay all the claims. Maintenance perils are excluded from property insurance policies because they either are certain to occur over time or are avoidable through regular maintenance and care.

7-4. An attitudinal hazard is carelessness or indifference to potential loss. Maintenance perils are those that are avoidable through regular maintenance and care. If policyholders were covered for maintenance perils, it might lead to an increasing carelessness regarding regular required maintenance to prevent loss.

Educational Objective 8

8-1. An example of a time element loss would be if a museum has extensive fire damage to its galleries, it would be unable to admit visitors and collect admission fees for several months.

8-2. The first item included in covered business income is the organization's net income (revenue minus expenses) that would have been earned if the insured property had not been damaged. The second item included in covered business income is the extra expenses that reduce the length of a business interruption or enable a business to continue some operations when the property has been damaged by a covered cause of loss.

8-3. Some extra expenses that would be covered for an insurance agent who wishes to conduct business at a temporary location during the repairs to his or her office building following a fire include rented office space, and any extra expenses (over and above her normal expenses) such as installing telephone service and notifying clients of the temporary location.

8-4. Some additional living expenses that would be covered for a homeowner whose home has been damaged include the following:
- Hotel room or furnished apartment
- Extra expense of eating at restaurants
- Boarding of pet(s)
- Extra expense of commuting further to work or school
- Washing clothes at a laundry rather than at home

Educational Objective 9

9-1. The persons or organizations with an insurable interest in property can include property owners, secured lenders, users of property, and other holders of property. Property insurance policies are written to cover these various interests in the following ways:
- The owner of a building is the named insured on a property insurance policy covering the building.
- A party that owns and occupies a building is the named insured on a policy covering both building and personal property.
- The tenant of a building is the named insured on a property insurance policy covering the tenant's personal property in that building.
- A secured lender, although usually not a named insured, is listed by name in the declarations (or in an endorsement) as a mortgagee or a loss payee.
- A bailee is the named insured on a bailee policy.

Educational Objective 10

10-1. The following rights are granted by the mortgage clause to a mortgagee who is named in the declarations of an insurance policy:
- The insurer promises to pay covered claims to both the named insured and the mortgagee as their interests appear (that is, to the extent of each party's insurable interest).
- The insurer promises to notify the mortgagee before any policy cancellation or nonrenewal enabling the mortgagee to replace the policy with other insurance.
- If the insurer cancels the policy and neglects to inform the mortgagee, the mortgagee's interest is still protected, even if the named insured no longer has coverage.
- The mortgagee has the right to pay the premium to the insurer if the insured fails to pay the premium to have the policy remain in effect.
- The mortgagee may file a claim for loss if the insured does not.
- The mortgagee may still collect under the policy if a claim is denied because the insured did not comply with the terms of the policy.

10-2. Two examples of coverage provided by a homeowners policy to parties who are neither named insureds nor secured lenders are (1) coverage for property owned by relatives and other persons under the age of twenty-one who reside in the named insured's household and (2) coverage for property belonging to guests, residence employees, and others while in the named insured's home.

10-3. Even though the fixtures are installed and made part of the building, Pradeep has an insurable interest in the fixtures. If he were forced to move to another apartment, he would have the expense of reinstalling them in another apartment. Pradeep might insure the fixtures under a tenant homeowners policy that covers the contents of his apartment.

Educational Objective 11

11-1. Insurance policies contain deductibles to encourage the insured to prevent losses and to enable the insurer to reduce premiums.

11-2. a. The policy limit specifies the maximum amount Radley may have to pay Atley for the damage.
   b. The deductible provision would reduce the amount Radley pays. Atley will bear the deductible portion of the loss.
   c. Unless Atley is underinsured, the insurance-to-value provisions will have no effect. If Atley is underinsured, the provision would reduce the amount Radley pays.
   d. The "other insurance" provision would not affect the amount Radley pays to Atley unless Atley also has other property insurance. In that case, other insurers with policies having the same terms, conditions, and provisions as Radley's policy would share the loss with Radley on a proportional basis. The total payments to Atley made by all the insurers will equal the loss and no more. Atley will not profit from the insured loss (principle of indemnity).

11-3. Insurance policies contain provisions designed to promote insurance to value by encouraging insureds to purchase an amount of insurance that is equal to, or close to, the value of the covered property, thus enabling insurers to provide property coverage at a fair rate.

Direct Your Learning

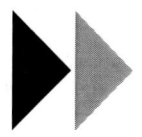

ASSIGNMENT 9

Liability Loss Exposures and Policy Provisions

Educational Objectives

After learning the content of this assignment, you should be able to:

1. Distinguish among the following:
   a. Constitutional law
   b. Statutory law
   c. Common law
2. Distinguish between criminal law and civil law.
3. Explain how each of the following can be the basis for legal liability:
   a. Torts
   b. Contracts
   c. Statutes
4. Describe the four elements of negligence.
5. Describe the potential financial consequences of liability loss exposures.
6. Describe circumstances that create liability loss exposures.
7. Identify the parties that may be insured by a liability insurance policy.
8. Describe the various types of injury or damage that are typically covered in liability insurance policies.
9. Describe loss exposures typically excluded in liability insurance policies.
10. Describe the costs typically covered in liability insurance policies and how these costs are determined.
11. Explain the difference between occurrence basis and claims-made coverage.
12. Explain how claim payments are affected by policy limits and defense cost provisions.
13. Define or describe each of the Key Words and Phrases for this assignment.

Study Materials

Required Reading:
▶ Property and Liability Insurance Principles
  • Chapter 9

Study Aids:
▶ SMART Online Practice Exams
▶ SMART Study Aids
  • Review Notes and Flash Cards—Assignment 9

Outline

- **Legal Liability**
  - A. Sources of Law
    1. Constitutional Law
    2. Statutory Law
    3. Common Law
  - B. Criminal Law Versus Civil Law
    1. Criminal Law
    2. Civil Law
    3. Criminal and Civil Consequences of the Same Act
- **Elements of a Liability Loss Exposure**
  - A. The Basis for Legal Liability
    1. Torts
    2. Contracts
    3. Statutes
  - B. Potential Financial Consequences of Liability Loss Exposures
    1. Damages
    2. Defense Costs
    3. Damage to Reputation
- **Categories of Liability Loss Exposures**
  - A. Automobiles and Other Conveyances
  - B. Premises
  - C. Business Operations
  - D. Completed Operations
  - E. Products
  - F. Advertising
  - G. Pollution
  - H. Liquor
  - I. Professional Activities
- **Liability Insurance Policy Provisions**
  - A. Covered Parties
  - B. Covered Activities
  - C. Covered Types of Injury or Damage
    1. Bodily Injury
    2. Property Damage
    3. Personal and Advertising Injury
  - D. Excluded Loss Exposures
  - E. Covered Costs
    1. Damages
    2. Defense Costs
    3. Supplementary Payments
    4. Medical Payments
  - F. Covered Time Period
    1. Occurrence Basis Coverage
    2. Claims-Made Coverage
  - G. Factors Affecting the Amount of Claim Payments
    1. Policy Limits
    2. Defense Cost Provisions
    3. "Other Insurance" Provisions
- **Summary**

study tips: Repetition helps students learn. Read, write, and repeat key points for each assignment.

For each assignment, you should define or describe each of the Key Words and Phrases and answer each of the Review and Application Questions.

Educational Objective 1

Distinguish among the following:

a. Constitutional law

b. Statutory law

c. Common law

Key Words and Phrases

Legal liability (p. 9.4)

Constitutional law (p. 9.4)

Statutory law (p. 9.5)

Common law, or case law (p. 9.5)

Review Questions

1-1. What are the sources of each of the following types of law? (p. 9.4)

   a. Constitutional law

b. Statutory law

c. Common law

1-2. List five fundamental rights guaranteed to United States citizens by amendments to the U.S. Constitution. (p. 9.4)

1-3. Provide four examples of government agencies that have regulatory powers derived from authority granted by legislative bodies. (p. 9.5)

Application Question

1-4. Insurance is governed by each state. States develop insurance regulations, determine how agents must be licensed, and control the insurance commerce in a state. Describe the source of law that is responsible for governing insurance and is therefore especially important in relation to insurance regulations. (p. 9.5)

Educational Objective 2
Distinguish between criminal law and civil law.

Key Words and Phrases

Criminal law (p. 9.6)

Civil law (p. 9.6)

Contract law (p. 9.6)

Review Questions

2-1. Illustrate the distinction between a criminal proceeding and a civil proceeding, giving an example of both. (pp. 9.6–9.7)

2-2. Identify the two types of rights civil law protects and provide an example of each. (pp. 9.6–9.7)

Application Question

2-3. Considering the types of actions that are punishable under criminal and civil law, under which category of law are the actions that generally become the subject of insurance claims? (pp. 9.6–9.7)

Educational Objective 3

Explain how each of the following can be the basis for legal liability:

a. Torts

b. Contracts

c. Statutes

Key Words and Phrases

Tort (p. 9.8)

Tort law (p. 9.8)

Negligence (p. 9.8)

Tortfeasor (p. 9.10)

Vicarious liability (p. 9.10)

Intentional tort (p. 9.10)

Assault (p. 9.10)

Battery (p. 9.10)

Defamation (p. 9.10)

Slander (p. 9.10)

Libel (p. 9.10)

False arrest (p. 9.10)

Invasion of privacy (p. 9.10)

Strict liability, or absolute liability (p. 9.11)

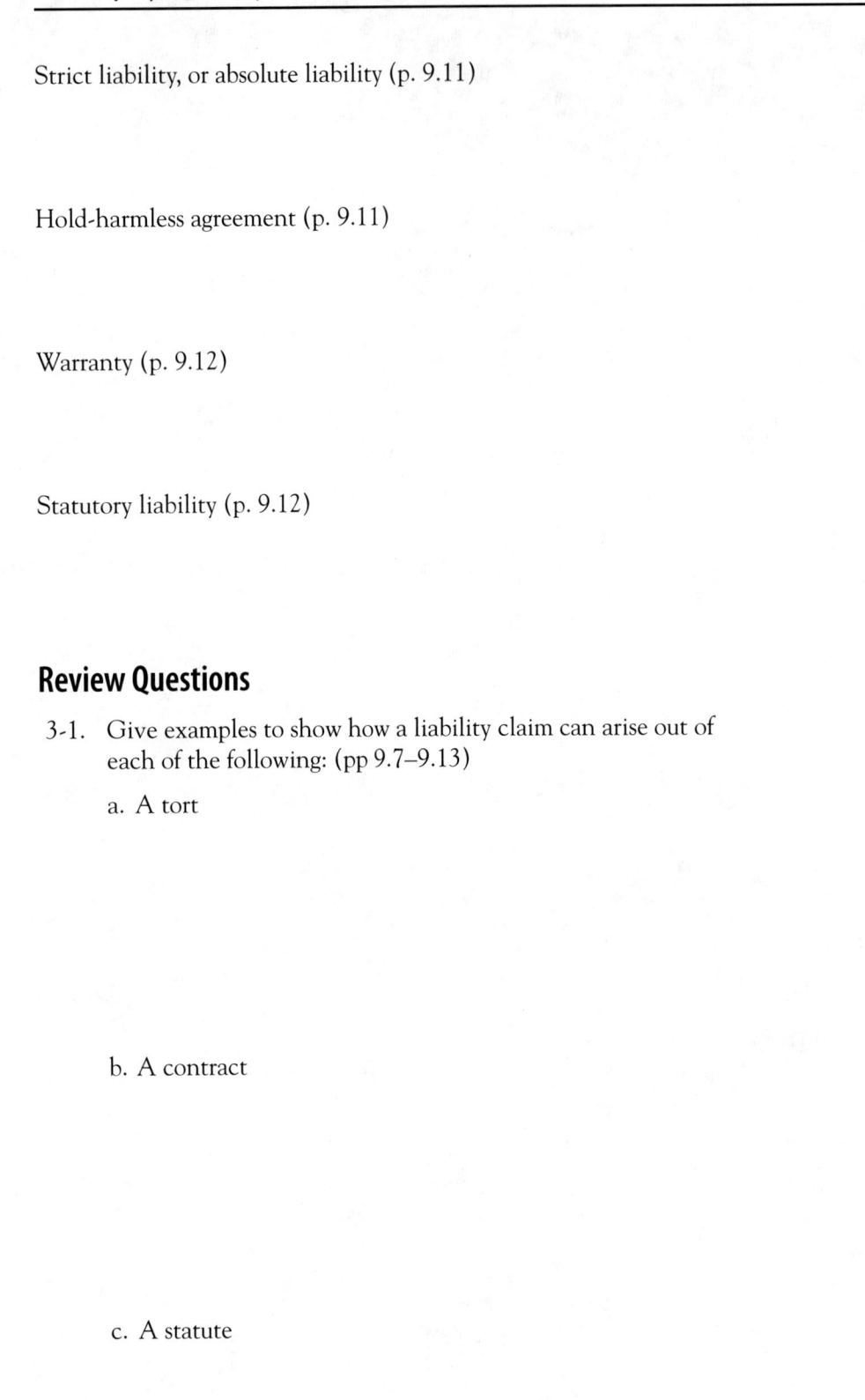

Hold-harmless agreement (p. 9.11)

Warranty (p. 9.12)

Statutory liability (p. 9.12)

Review Questions

3-1. Give examples to show how a liability claim can arise out of each of the following: (pp 9.7–9.13)

   a. A tort

   b. A contract

   c. A statute

3-2. Identify the two aspects of contract law that give an injured party the legal basis for recovering damages from another party. (p. 9.11)

3-3. Identify two insurance-related statutes that give an injured party the legal basis for recovering damages from another party. (p. 9.12)

Application Question

3-4. Tony rented a car for a vacation. While he was on vacation, he ran a red light and struck another vehicle. He was found to have been driving while under the influence of alcohol and his driver's license was suspended. Tony's insurer is making payments to the other driver for injuries and damage to the driver's vehicle. In addition, the rental car company charged Tony's credit card for the damages to the rental vehicle and for its loss of use. Differentiate the various legal bases for damages that have occurred in this case. (pp. 9.8–9.13)

Educational Objective 4

Describe the four elements of negligence.

Review Questions

4-1. The floor in the dairy section of a supermarket was wet because it had just been mopped. A customer, Gerald, slipped and fell, breaking his ankle. How did each of the four elements of negligence apply in this situation? (pp. 9.8–9.9)

4-2. Based on vicarious liability, how can a person become liable for another's actions? (p. 9.10)

4-3. Some intentional torts are covered by the personal injury coverage of liability insurance policies. List six intentional torts. (p. 9.10)

4-4. How can a person transfer his or her liability to another party by using a contract? (pp. 9.11–9.12)

4-5. Using either auto no-fault laws or workers' compensation insurance as an example, explain how legal liability can be imposed by a statute or law. (p. 9.12)

Application Questions

4-6. A cosmetic manufacturer failed to conduct adequate allergy testing on a new line of cosmetics before marketing it as "the complete system of hypoallergenic skin care." Marie bought the cosmetics only to experience a severe allergic reaction that required emergency medical care and a slow, painful recovery. Describe two distinct principles of law on which Marie could base a suit against the cosmetic manufacturer. (pp. 9.8–9.9)

4-7. Steve is employed as a delivery truck driver for a furniture company. While making a delivery, Steve carelessly drove across the highway center line and collided with another vehicle, injuring its driver. (pp. 9.8–9.10)

   a. Will the injured driver be legally entitled to obtain compensation on the basis of negligence? If so, briefly describe the four elements of negligence that would need to be present, relating each element to Steve's accident.

   b. Explain the potential significance of vicarious liability to the accident.

Educational Objective 5

Describe the potential financial consequences of liability loss exposures.

Review Questions

5-1. Compare damages and defense costs. (pp. 9.13–9.14)

5-2. Identify the three types of damages that could be awarded by a court. (p. 9.13)

5-3. Provide examples of expenses that are covered by defense costs. (p. 9.14)

Application Question

5-4. Most liability insurance policies pay for defense costs in addition to the limit of coverage for damages. However, some liability policies pay for defense costs within the limit of coverage for damages. Explain why it would be to the insured's advantage to have the former, rather than the latter, type of liability insurance policy. (pp. 9.13–9.14)

Educational Objective 6
Describe circumstances that create liability loss exposures.

Key Word or Phrase
Liability insurance (p. 9.17)

Review Questions

6-1. List nine different kinds of business or professional activities that can lead to a liability loss. (pp. 9.14–9.17)

6-2. What are some basic differences in the nature of liability insurance and property insurance? (p. 9.17)

Application Question

6-3. Gallon Corporation owns a factory building in which it manufactures small household appliances. Gallon owns the trucks that are used to deliver these appliances to the Gallon retail outlets where they are sold. (pp. 9.14–9.17)

   a. Identify three activities or situations that could create liability loss exposures for Gallon.

b. Describe two of the possible financial consequences for Gallon if a liability loss results from any of the activities or situations identified in your answer to a. above.

Educational Objective 7
Identify the parties that may be insured by a liability insurance policy.

Review Questions

7-1. Give four examples of a party other than the named insured who may be covered under a liability insurance policy.
(p. 9.18)

7-2. Identify a type of policy that is an example of general liability insurance and describe what this policy essentially covers.
(p. 9.19)

Application Question

7-3. Smith owns an appliance store and has purchased liability insurance coverage that applies to this business. Other than Smith, what people or organizations may be covered by this liability insurance? (pp. 9.18–9.19)

Educational Objective 8
Describe the various types of injury or damage that are typically covered in liability insurance policies.

Key Words and Phrases

Bodily injury (p. 9.19)

Property damage (p. 9.20)

Personal injury (p. 9.20)

Review Questions

8-1. What is the difference between "bodily injury" and "personal injury" as those terms are used in liability insurance policies? (pp. 9.19–9.21)

8-2. Describe the two types of losses incurred as a result of property damage. (p. 9.20)

8-3. The definitions of personal injury offenses and advertising injury offenses overlap somewhat. Does this overlap result in duplicate coverage? Explain. (p. 9.21)

Application Question

8-4. Sam owns a plumbing company. He has a staff of four plumbers and an administrative assistant who completes the bookwork, answers telephone calls, and dispatches the plumbers to job sites. Provide an example of how Sam's plumbing company may incur liability losses for the following types of injury or damage: (pp. 9.19–9.21)

   a. Bodily injury

   b. Property damage

c. Personal injury

d. Advertising injury

Educational Objective 9
Describe loss exposures typically excluded in liability insurance policies.

Review Questions

9-1. List six categories of exclusions found in liability insurance policies. (pp. 9.21–9.22)

9-2. Provide an example of an exclusion designed to avoid insuring preventable losses. (p. 9.21)

Application Question

9-3. Stan owns a 1970 Pontiac GTO that he occasionally drives to work. On weekends, he likes to take the GTO to the gatherings of his racing club, where he and other amateurs can race their vintage muscle cars. Stan was dismayed to learn that his personal auto policy would not cover his racing activities. As Stan's insurance agent, how would you justify this policy exclusion? (pp. 9.21–9.22)

Educational Objective 10

Describe the costs typically covered in liability insurance policies and how these costs are determined.

Key Words and Phrases

Supplementary payments (p. 9.25)

Prejudgment interest (p. 9.25)

Postjudgment interest (p. 9.25)

Medical payments coverage (p. 9.25)

Review Questions

10-1. What damages are covered by a typical liability insurance policy? (pp. 9.22–9.23)

10-2. Do most liability insurance claims involve a court trial? Explain why or why not. (pp. 9.23–9.24)

10-3. In addition to the payment of any damages for which the insured becomes legally responsible, what additional costs are covered by a typical liability insurance policy? (pp. 9.24–9.25)

10-4. How does the medical payments coverage of a typical liability insurance policy differ from the liability coverage under the same policy? (p. 9.25)

Application Question

10-5. The roof on a house recently constructed for the Jones family by a building company collapsed, and several members of the Jones family were injured. Identify and describe two types of damages that may be awarded to the injured members of the Jones family as the result of their liability claims against the building company. (pp. 9.22–9.23)

Educational Objective 11
Explain the difference between occurrence basis and claims-made coverage.

Key Words and Phrases

Occurrence basis coverage (p. 9.26)

Claims-made coverage (p. 9.26)

Retroactive date (p. 9.27)

Review Questions

11-1. What is the distinction between claims-made coverage and occurrence basis coverage? (pp. 9.26–9.27)

11-2. Explain how occurrence policies provide an advantage to insureds while, at the same time, provide a disadvantage to insurers. (p. 9.26)

11-3. Explain how the retroactive date in claims-made policies can affect coverage. (p. 9.27)

Educational Objective 12
Explain how claim payments are affected by policy limits and defense cost provisions.

Key Words and Phrases
Each person limit (p. 9.27)

Each occurrence limit (p. 9.27)

Aggregate limit (p. 9.27)

Split limits (p. 9.28)

Single limit (p. 9.28)

Review Questions

12-1. Identify the three policy provisions that determine an insurer's payment on a liability claim. (p. 9.27)

12-2. Explain how claim payments are affected by the following limits. (p. 9.27)

   a. Each person limit

   b. Each occurrence limit

   c. Aggregate limit

12-3. How is an insurer's payment for defense costs affected by policy limits? (p. 9.29)

Answers to Assignment 9 Questions

NOTE: These answers are provided to give students a basic understanding of acceptable types of responses. They often are not the only valid answers and are not intended to provide an exhaustive response to the questions.

Educational Objective 1

1-1.   a.   The source of constitutional law is the U.S. Constitution.
   b.   The sources of statutory law are legislative bodies.
   c.   The sources of common law are court decisions.

1-2.   The U.S. Constitution, by its amendments guarantees all citizens freedom of speech, freedom of religion, freedom from unreasonable searches and seizures, the right to trial by jury, and the right to due process of law.

1-3.   Four examples of government agencies that have regulatory powers derived from authority granted by legislative bodies are the Federal Trade Commission, the Environmental Protection Agency, state public utility commissions, and local zoning boards.

1-4.   Statutory law is developed at the federal, state, or local level. Through statutory law, each state grants regulatory powers to the office of an insurance commissioner who oversees the operation of insurance within the state.

Educational Objective 2

2-1.
- Example of criminal proceeding: A driver in a stolen car runs a stop sign, hitting another car and killing a passenger. The government prosecutes the driver for motor vehicle homicide. Society deems homicide so harmful to the public welfare that the government takes the responsibility for prosecuting and punishing the accused offender.
- Example of civil proceeding: The family of the passenger who was killed initiates a lawsuit against the driver on the passenger's behalf for monetary damages from wrongful death. Wrongful death is not governed by criminal law.

2-2.   One right civil law protects is personal and property rights. For example, if someone invades the privacy or property of another person or harms another's reputation, the injured person can seek amends in court. A second right civil law protects is contract rights. For example, if two parties make a contract that one party does not honor, the other party can ask the court to compel adherence to the contract or to assess damages.

2-3.   Insurance claims generally fall under civil law—this category of law deals with the rights and responsibilities of citizens with respect to one another. These rights and responsibilities are often the legal basis for a claim by one party against another for damages.

Educational Objective 3

3-1. a. A tort is any wrongful act, other than a crime or breach of contract, committed by one party against another. An individual or organization can face a claim for legal liability on the basis of negligence, intentional torts, or strict liability. For example, a shopowner does not shovel snow from the sidewalk in front of her shop. A passerby slips and falls on this snow-covered sidewalk and sustains extensive injuries. The injured passerby may sue the shopowner for negligence and collect damages.

b. A contract is a legally enforceable agreement between two or more parties. Parties to a contract sometimes find it convenient for one party to assume the financial consequences of certain types of liability faced by the other. For example, the owner of a building may enter into a contract with a contractor who makes a contract with a subcontractor to accept responsibility for certain actions of the subcontractor. If the subcontractor's actions injure a customer and the customer sues the building owner, the contractor will pay any damages owed.

c. A statute is a law. Statutory liability is legal liability imposed by a specific statute or law. For example, no-fault auto laws modify some common-law principles of negligence that apply to auto accidents.

3-2. The two aspects of contract law that give an injured party the legal basis for recovering damages from another party are liability assumed under contract and breach of warranty.

3-3. Two statutes that give an injured party the legal basis for recovering damages from another party are no-fault auto laws and workers' compensation laws.

3-4. The various legal bases for the damages in this case are as follows:
- The payments to the other driver are based on tort laws—in this case, negligence.
- The suspension of Tony's driver's license could have been the result of a statute in the state in which Tony was driving. Many states have enacted statutes governing the punishments associated with a DUI conviction.
- The charge against Tony's credit card by the rental car company was based on contract law. The lease of a rental car includes stipulations regarding payment for damage or loss of use of the rented vehicle.

Educational Objective 4

4-1.
- The element of negligence, duty owed to another, applies. The supermarket owes its customers safe building conditions.
- The element of negligence, a breach of that duty, applies. The supermarket was negligent for having an employee mop the floor and not roping off the unsafe area from its customers.
- The element of negligence, injury or damage, applies. Gerald was injured when he slipped, fell, and broke his ankle.
- The element of negligence, unbroken chain of events between the breach of duty and the injury or damage, applies. Gerald broke his ankle when he fell because he slipped on the wet floor, because the supermarket did not rope off the wet and slippery area from its customers, and because an employee mopped the floor.

4-2. An employer can be vicariously liable for the actions of an employee performing work-related activities on behalf of the employer.

4-3. Six intentional torts are as follows:
- Assault
- Battery
- Libel
- Slander
- False arrest
- Invasion of privacy

4-4. A hold-harmless agreement can obligate one party to assume the legal liability of another party.

4-5. A workers' compensation statute imposes automatic (strict) liability on the employer to pay specified benefits and eliminates an employee's right to sue the employer for most work-related injuries. As long as the injury is work-related, the employer pays the employee the benefits specified in the law regardless of who is at fault.

4-6. Marie could base a suit against the cosmetic manufacturer on the following principles of law:
- Negligence—The cosmetic manufacturer failed to conduct adequate allergy testing on its new line of cosmetics before marketing it and thereby breached a duty owed to its customers. This breach of duty resulted in Marie's severe allergic reaction. Marie should be able to prove that an unbroken chain of events exists from breach of duty to severe allergic reaction.
- Breach of warranty—The company's slogan, in effect, was a warranty that no allergic reaction would result.

4-7. a. The four elements of negligence are (1) a duty owed to another, (2) a breach of that duty, (3) definite injury or damage to the other person, and (4) an unbroken chain of events leading from the breach of duty to the injury. All four elements of negligence are apparent in the case of Steve's accident: (1) Steve had a duty to other drivers to operate his vehicle in a safe manner; (2) Steve's failure to stay in his lane of the road was a breach of that duty; (3) the other driver was injured; and (4) the other driver's injury resulted, in an unbroken chain of events, from Steve's breach of duty.
   b. Because Steve was acting on behalf of his employer at the time of the accident, the employer can be held responsible for Steve's negligence. This kind of responsibility is known as vicarious liability.

Educational Objective 5

5-1. Damages are paid to compensate the victim because of liability for injury or damage. Defense costs are paid to defend the alleged wrongdoer.

5-2. The three types of damages that a court could award are special damages, general damages, and punitive damages. Special damages and general damages are compensatory damages.

5-3. Some examples of expenses that are covered by defense costs include the fees paid to lawyers and all expenses associated with defending a liability claim, such as investigation expenses, expert witness fees, premiums for necessary bonds, and other expenses incurred to prepare for and conduct a trial.

5-4. Defense costs can exhaust the limit of liability that a policyholder may carry on a policy. It is a significant benefit to have defense costs paid in addition to the limit of liability coverage, which can then be used to pay for any judgments made against the insured.

Educational Objective 6

6-1. Business or professional activities that can lead to a liability loss may include any of the following:
- Automobiles and other conveyances—Businesses owning delivery trucks are responsible for accidents involving their trucks.
- Premises—Property owners can be held responsible for injuries on their premises.
- Business operations—Liability issues can occur on or off premises.
- Completed operations—A liability loss exposure remains for persons or businesses after completing a job and leaving the work site.
- Products—Manufacturers are responsible for products they produce that cause bodily injury or property damage.
- Advertising—Businesses can be liable for using the materials of others (pictures, text, trademarks, and slogans) without permission.
- Pollution—Liability can arise from the manufacture, use, or disposal of environmental contaminants.
- Liquor—Providers of alcohol can be responsible for customers or guests who become intoxicated and injure someone while driving drunk.
- Professional activities—Professional liability arises if injury or damage can be attributed to a professional's failure to exercise the appropriate standard of care.

6-2. Basic differences in the nature of property insurance and liability insurance include the following:
- Property insurance claims usually involve only two parties—the insurer and the insured. Liability claims involve three parties—the insurer, the insured, and a third party who is the claimant.
- Property insurance claims are paid to an insured when covered property is damaged by a covered cause of loss during the policy period. Liability insurance claims are paid to a third party on behalf of an insured against whom a claim has been made, provided the claim is covered by the policy.
- Property insurance policies must clarify which property and cause of loss the policy covers. Liability insurance policies must indicate the activities and types of injury or damage that are covered.

6-3. a. The following could create a liability loss for Gallon:
- An employee could be injured while performing a work-related task.
- A customer could be injured by a defective manufactured appliance.
- A customer's house could be damaged during a delivery.

b. The following could be possible financial consequences of a liability loss for Gallon:
- Medical costs, estimates for pain and suffering, and lost wages for the employee
- Medical costs, estimates for pain and suffering, lost wages for the customer, and cost to replace defective appliance
- Cost to repair or replace the customer's damaged property

Educational Objective 7

7-1. Individuals other than the named insured who may be covered under a liability insurance policy include the following:
- Relatives of the named insured or spouse, if the relatives reside in the household
- Persons under twenty-one and in the care of an insured
- Any person or organization legally responsible for animals or watercraft owned by an insured (except in business situations)
- Employees using a covered vehicle, such as a lawn tractor, and other people using a covered vehicle on an insured location with the named insured's consent

7-2. An example of general liability insurance is a commercial general liability policy (CGL policy). This policy essentially covers those claims that are not excluded and specifically excludes coverage for claims that are better handled by specific liability insurance policies, such as automobile liability, workers' compensation, aircraft and watercraft liability, and professional liability.

7-3. The parties who are afforded liability coverage because of their business relationship to the named insured include the following:
- Employees of the named insured
- Real estate managers for the named insured
- Persons responsible for the property of a named insured who has died
- Any organization that is newly acquired or formed by the named insured for up to a certain number of days after it is acquired or formed.

Educational Objective 8

8-1. In liability insurance policies "bodily injury" and "personal injury" are differentiated in the following way:
- Bodily injury is any physical injury to a person, including sickness, disease, and death. Personal injury in insurance is usually used to mean injury, other than bodily injury, arising from intentional torts such as libel, slander, or invasion of privacy. A few policies define personal injury to include bodily injury, as well as libel, slander, and other offenses.

8-2. Types of loss incurred as a result of property damage include (1) a direct loss, such as a fire at a grocery store, and (2) a time element (or indirect) loss, such as if the fire at the grocery store causes indirect damage to the owners of surrounding businesses because they have to cease operations temporarily.

8-3. The definition overlap between personal injury offenses and advertising injury offenses does not result in duplicate coverage. Current versions of the CGL policy include both personal and advertising injury in the same insuring agreement, so no coverage duplication results from repeating that a certain type of claim is covered.

8-4. Sam's plumbing company may incur liability losses for the following:
   a. Bodily injury—One of the plumbers hits a pedestrian with a plumbing truck while traveling to a job site.
   b. Property damage—The repairs made at a job site fail and water floods the floor of an office building during the night.

c. Personal injury—The administrative assistant makes a false comment to others in the community indicating a customer is not paying the plumbing company's bills.

d. Advertising injury—Sam lists the names of satisfied customers in his newspaper advertisement without obtaining their consent.

Educational Objective 9

9-1. The six categories of exclusions found in liability insurance policies are to avoid covering "uninsurable" losses, to avoid insuring losses that could be prevented, to eliminate duplicate coverage, to eliminate coverage that most insureds do not need, to eliminate coverage for exposures that require special handling by the insurer, and to keep premiums reasonable.

9-2. An example would be an exclusion for losses that can be prevented by avoiding illegal activity, such as losses resulting from the possession of controlled substances.

9-3. Stan's agent may point out that most individuals are not involved in racing, and providing such coverage would add costs to the majority of insureds who do not need that coverage.

Educational Objective 10

10-1. A typical liability insurance policy covers the following damages:
- Special damages—compensation for hospital bills, physicians' fees, lost income, and rehabilitation expenses
- General damages—compensation for pain and suffering
- Punitive damages, if stated—punishment for outrageous conduct (Some states do not permit insurers to pay punitive damages claims.)

10-2. No. Very few liability claims are decided by the courts. Most are settled out of court before the claimant files a lawsuit. Out-of-court settlements resolve cases quickly and eliminate uncertainty about the outcome of a claim.

10-3. A typical liability insurance policy covers the following additional costs:
- Defense costs, such as attorneys' fees and expenses, investigation, legal research, and expert witness fees
- Supplementary payments, such as the insured's loss of earnings while attending hearings or trials at the insurer's request
- Prejudgment and postjudgment interest
- Medical payments coverage

10-4. Medical payments coverage of a typical liability insurance policy generally pays necessary medical expenses incurred within a specified period by a claimant for a covered injury, regardless of whether the insured was at fault. Liability coverage is paid only if the insured was at fault.

10-5. Damages that may be awarded to injured members of the Jones family as a result of their liability claims against the building company include the following compensatory damages:
- Special damages—hospital costs, doctor fees, miscellaneous medical expenses, and lost wages for time spent away from the job during recovery
- General damages—an estimated dollar value related to pain and suffering; disfigurement; loss of limbs, sight, or hearing; and loss of the ability to bear children

Educational Objective 11

11-1. • Occurrence basis coverage covers liability claims that occur during the policy period, regardless of when the claim is submitted to the insurer.

• Claims-made coverage covers liability claims that are first made (submitted) during the policy period for covered events that occur on or after the retroactive date and before the end of the policy period.

11-2. Occurrence policies are advantageous to insureds because they offer valuable protection for unknown and unforeseen claims. For insurers, however, occurrence coverage means that liability claims may surface long after a policy has expired.

11-3. The retroactive date in claims-made policies can affect coverage because claims based on injuries that occur before the retroactive date are not covered, even if the claim is made during the policy period. Also, an insured who replaces a claims-made policy with another claims-made policy with a new retroactive date may face a gap in coverage.

Educational Objective 12

12-1. The three policy provisions that determine an insurer's payment on a liability claim are policy limits, defense cost provisions, and "other insurance" provisions.

12-2. a. Under an each person limit, the claim amount may be affected by the maximum amount an insurer will pay for injury to any one person.

b. Under an each occurrence limit, the claim amount may be affected by the maximum amount an insurer will pay for all covered losses from a single occurrence, regardless of the number of persons injured or the number of parties claiming property damage.

c. Under an aggregate limit, the claim amount may be affected by the maximum amount an insurer will pay for all covered losses during the covered period, which is usually the same as the policy period.

12-3. The insurer usually is not obligated to provide further defense once the entire policy limit has been paid in settlement or judgment for damages.

Direct Your Learning

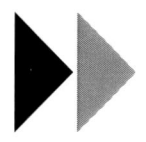

Assignment 10

Managing Loss Exposures: Risk Management

Educational Objectives

After learning the content of this assignment, you should be able to:

1. Describe the six steps in the risk management process.
2. Describe three primary methods of identifying loss exposures.
3. Explain why measuring loss frequency and loss severity is important in analyzing loss exposures.
4. Describe the risk management techniques of risk control and risk financing.
5. Describe the financial criteria and guidelines for selecting risk management techniques.
6. Describe procedures for implementing risk management techniques.
7. Describe procedures for monitoring and revising a risk management program.
8. Explain the benefits of sound risk management.
9. Given a case, recommend risk management techniques appropriate for an individual, a family, or a business.
10. Define or describe each of the Key Words and Phrases for this assignment.

Study Materials

Required Reading:
- Property and Liability Insurance Principles
  - Chapter 10

Study Aids:
- SMART Online Practice Exams
- SMART Study Aids
  - Review Notes and Flash Cards—Assignment 10

Outline

▶ **The Risk Management Process**
  A. Step 1: Identifying Loss Exposures
     1. Physical Inspection
     2. Loss Exposure Surveys
     3. Loss Histories
  B. Step 2: Analyzing Loss Exposures
     1. Loss Frequency
     2. Loss Severity
  C. Step 3: Examining the Feasibility of Risk Management Techniques
     1. Risk Control
     2. Risk Financing
  D. Step 4: Selecting the Appropriate Risk Management Techniques
     1. Decisions Based on Financial Criteria
     2. Decisions Based on Informal Guidelines
  E. Step 5: Implementing the Selected Risk Management Techniques
     1. Deciding What Should Be Done
     2. Deciding Who Should Be Responsible
     3. Communicating Risk Management Information
     4. Allocating Costs of the Risk Management Program
  F. Step 6: Monitoring Results and Revising the Risk Management Program

▶ **Benefits of Risk Management**
  A. Benefits of Risk Management to Businesses
  B. Benefits of Risk Management to Individuals and Families
  C. Benefits of Risk Management to Society
  D. Benefits of Risk Management to Insurers

▶ **An Example of a Risk Management Program**

▶ **Summary**

Study tips: Set aside a specific, realistic amount of time to study every day.

For each assignment, you should define or describe each of the Key Words and Phrases and answer each of the Review and Application Questions.

> ## Educational Objective 1
> Describe the six steps in the risk management process.

Key Word or Phrase

Risk management (p. 10.3)

Review Questions

1-1. Define the goal of risk management. (p. 10.4)

1-2. Is risk management performed only by risk managers? Explain. (p. 10.4)

1-3. What are the six steps in the risk management process? (pp. 10.4–10.16)

Application Question

1-4. Considering your own automobile or an automobile of a friend of yours, explain how you would apply the risk management process to the physical damage exposures of that vehicle? (pp. 10.4–10.16)

Educational Objective 2
Describe three primary methods of identifying loss exposures.

Review Questions

2-1. What are three methods that can be used for identifying loss exposures? (pp. 10.4–10.7)

2-2. Describe an advantage and a disadvantage of a loss exposure survey. (p. 10.5)

Application Question

2-3. Assume that you have purchased a shop that repairs lawnmowers. Describe the method(s) you would use to identify the loss exposures at the shop, and explain how you would apply these chosen methods. (pp. 10.4–10.7)

Educational Objective 3

Explain why measuring loss frequency and loss severity is important in analyzing loss exposures.

Key Words and Phrases

Loss frequency (p. 10.7)

Loss severity (p. 10.7)

Review Questions

3-1. What does a risk manager need to measure when analyzing loss exposures? (pp. 10.7–10.8)

3-2. Explain why accurate measurement of loss frequency is important in analyzing loss exposures. (p. 10.7)

3-3. Explain why accurate measurement of loss severity is important in analyzing loss exposures. (pp. 10.7–10.8)

Application Question

3-4. When underwriters review past losses, they are concerned about the frequency and the severity of losses. They often pay close attention to the number of losses that a business or homeowner has experienced, even if the losses have been small or resulted in no payment. Explain why an underwriter may pay such close attention to the frequency of losses. (pp. 10.7–10.8)

Educational Objective 4

Describe the risk management techniques of risk control and risk financing.

Key Words and Phrases

Risk control (p. 10.8)

Avoidance (p. 10.8)

Loss prevention (p. 10.9)

Loss reduction (p. 10.9)

Separation (p. 10.9)

Duplication (p. 10.9)

Risk financing (p. 10.10)

Retention (p. 10.10)

Noninsurance transfer (p. 10.10)

Review Questions

4-1. What happens to loss probability when a loss exposure is avoided? (p. 10.8)

4-2. How do insurers' inspection reports lead insureds to implement loss control measures? (p. 10.9)

4-3. Give an example of each of the following: (p. 10.10)

   a. Unintentional retention

   b. Intentional retention

   c. Partial retention

4-4. How does a hold-harmless agreement transfer the financial consequences of a loss exposure without using insurance? (pp. 10.10–10.11)

4-5. What happens to loss exposures when the risk management technique of insurance is used? (p. 10.11)

Application Question

4-6. The mere presence of a burglar alarm keeps some burglaries from happening and limits the size of loss when a burglary occurs. Why? First, burglars prefer to steal from buildings with no alarm. Second, when a burglar sets off an alarm, the burglar often leaves quickly without stealing very much. Using this example, distinguish between loss prevention and loss reduction, and explain why a burglar alarm may be considered both a loss prevention measure and a loss reduction measure. (p. 10.9)

Educational Objective 5
Describe the financial criteria and guidelines for selecting risk management techniques.

Review Questions

5-1. What financial criteria can be used in making risk management decisions? (p. 10.13)

5-2. What four informal guidelines are useful in making risk management decisions? (pp. 10.13–10.14)

5-3. Describe what occurs when insurance takes the place of loss control, and provide a more economical approach to risk management. (p. 10.13–10.14)

Application Question

5-4. As treasurer for a limousine company, Chris is responsible for buying the firm's insurance. After tracing increased expenses to an increased frequency in physical damage losses to the firm's fleet of limousines, Chris instructs the firm's insurance agent to decrease the $1,000 per car physical damage deductible to $100 per car. (p. 10.14)

   a. What informal guideline has Chris ignored?

   b. What could Chris have done to address the increased loss frequency instead of decreasing the deductible?

Educational Objective 6
Describe procedures for implementing risk management techniques.

Review Questions

6-1. What decisions must a risk manager make to implement chosen risk management techniques? (p. 10.15)

6-2. Explain whether risk managers usually have complete authority to implement risk management techniques. (p. 10.15)

6-3. Explain how risk management departments of large organizations communicate risk management information. (p. 10.15)

Educational Objective 7
Describe procedures for monitoring and revising a risk management program.

Review Questions

7-1. How should a risk management program be monitored? (p. 10.16)

7-2. Briefly describe what monitoring a risk management program entails. (p. 10.16)

7-3. Why should a household or an organization thoroughly review its insurance program with its agent or broker each year? (p. 10.16)

Application Question

7-4. James has implemented a set of loss control measures at a grocery store to create a safer environment for the shoppers in that store. Explain how James should monitor and modify his risk management program. (p. 10.16)

Educational Objective 8
Explain the benefits of sound risk management.

Review Questions

8-1. How can a business benefit from risk management? (p. 10.17)

8-2. How can individuals and families benefit from risk management? (pp. 10.17–10.18)

8-3. How does society as a whole benefit from risk management? (p. 10.18)

8-4. How do insurers benefit from risk management? (p. 10.18)

Application Question

8-5. Assume that you are the head of a family household. Your teenage son has just purchased his first vehicle and is questioning the value of purchasing insurance. He is complaining that it is too expensive and he can afford only minimum limits. Apply the benefits of risk management to individuals and families to encourage him to purchase adequate insurance coverage. (pp. 10.17–10.18)

Educational Objective 9

Given a case, recommend risk management techniques appropriate for an individual, a family, or a business.

Review Questions

9-1. How did the Garcia family in the textbook use each of the steps in the risk management process? (pp. 10.19–10.20)

   a. Identify loss exposures

   b. Analyze loss exposures

   c. Examine the feasibility of risk management techniques

   d. Select appropriate risk management techniques

e. Implement the selected techniques

f. Monitor and revise the risk management program

9-2. Why did the Garcia family decide not to specifically insure their daughter's saxophone? (p. 10.20)

9-3. How would the Garcia family apply the retention technique if their daughter were to lose or damage her saxophone? (p. 10.20)

Managing Loss Exposures: Risk Management   10.17

Answers to Assignment 10 Questions

NOTE: These answers are provided to give students a basic understanding of acceptable types of responses. They often are not the only valid answers and are not intended to provide an exhaustive response to the questions.

Educational Objective 1

1-1. The goal of risk management is to minimize the adverse effects of loss exposures by reducing the frequency and severity of losses.

1-2. The person who performs the risk management function differs, depending on the household or organization. While the responsible person in an organization may be an employee known as the risk manager, in other organizations, risk management may be performed by someone outside the firm—for example, a risk management consultant. In a household, the person who performs risk management may be the primary wage earner or the person who handles the household finances.

1-3. The six steps in the risk management process include the following:
- Identifying loss exposures
- Analyzing loss exposures
- Examining the feasibility of risk management techniques
- Selecting the appropriate risk management techniques
- Implementing the selected risk management techniques
- Monitoring the results and revising the risk management program

1-4. Applying the risk management process to physical damages exposures of an automobile involves the following stages:
- Identifying loss exposures:
  - Determine where the vehicle is parked at night and the exposures at that location
  - Determine the route used to commute to work or school and the hazards along the route
- Analyzing loss exposures:
  - Determine the driving record of the drivers and their potential for future losses
- Examining the feasibility of risk management techniques:
  - Avoidance—Sell the car
  - Loss control—Use a parking garage, go to driving school, or drive on a safer route
  - Retention—Assume responsibility for loss or select a large deductible
  - Noninsurance transfer—Ride a taxi
  - Insurance—Purchase a policy
- Selecting the appropriate risk management technique:
  - Probably purchase a policy and increase the deductible
- Implementing the selected risk management technique
  - Shop for the best price for the coverage available on an insurance policy
- Monitoring results and revising the risk management program:
  - Make sure the loss exposures do not change and the coverage remains affordable

Educational Objective 2

2-1. Three methods that can be used to identify loss exposures include the following:
- Physical inspection
- Loss exposure survey
- Loss histories

2-2. A loss exposure survey can be a valuable tool to help the risk manager identify the organization's loss exposures. If used appropriately, the survey also familiarizes the risk manager with all the organization's operations. The survey's major weakness is that it may omit an important loss exposure, especially if the organization has unique operations not included on a standard survey form.

2-3. Methods to identify loss exposures include the following:
- Physical inspection—Look around the shop for dangers to customers as well as to workers.
- Loss exposure survey—You might use a loss exposure survey designed for power equipment stores to identify exposures that you have overlooked.
- Loss histories—Review records on past losses, recognizing that anything that has happened in the past can happen again.

Educational Objective 3

3-1. A risk manager should measure the likely frequency and likely severity of a potential loss when analyzing loss exposures.

3-2. Accurate measurement of loss frequency is important in analyzing loss exposures because the proper treatment of the loss exposure often depends on how frequently the loss is expected to occur. If a particular type of loss occurs frequently, or if its frequency has been increasing in recent years, the risk manager may decide that procedures for controlling losses are necessary to decrease the frequency of loss.

3-3. Accurate measurement of loss severity is important in analyzing loss exposures because the potential severity of losses is a major consideration in determining whether the household or organization should insure a particular loss exposure or retain all or part of the potential financial consequences of the loss exposure.

3-4. Underwriters pay close attention to the frequency of losses for the following several reasons:
- A trend in losses can indicate a future pattern.
- Any loss may become a severe loss, given the right circumstances.

Educational Objective 4

4-1. When a loss exposure is avoided, the probability of loss from this loss exposure is zero—there is no probability of loss. However, avoidance of this loss exposure may pose other problems.

4-2. As a result of an insurer's inspection report, underwriters may require the applicant to implement the loss control before the insurer is willing to accept the application.

4-3. a. Unintentional retention occurs if a restaurant does not identify its liability exposure for serving too much alcohol to a customer and fails to purchase liquor liability insurance to cover this exposure.

b. Intentional retention occurs if a delivery company owning very old trucks retains its exposure for collision losses and pays for any collision losses from the company's operating funds.

c. Partial retention occurs if an individual wanting a lower auto insurance premium intentionally chooses a $500 deductible on a personal auto policy.

4-4. A hold-harmless agreement transfers potential financial consequences of a loss exposure from one party to another party that is not an insurer. For example, a landlord can use a hold-harmless agreement to transfer its liability exposure to the tenant.

4-5. Insurance transfers financial consequences of specified losses from one party (the insured) to an insurer in exchange for a specified fee (premium). For example, a family purchases homeowners and personal auto policies from an insurer to transfer its property and liability exposures.

4-6.
- Loss prevention is lowering the loss frequency by reducing the number of losses. Burglars may avoid buildings that have burglar alarms. Other burglars may become frightened by the alarm, leave immediately, and steal nothing.
- Loss reduction is lowering the loss severity by reducing the dollar amount of losses. Burglars may be alerted by the alarm, leave sooner than they would have if the alarm had not sounded, and steal less.

Educational Objective 5

5-1. The following financial criteria can be used in making risk management decisions:
- Increasing profits
- Increasing operating efficiency

5-2. Four informal guidelines useful in making risk management decisions include the following:
- Do not retain more than you can afford to lose.
- Do not retain large exposures to save a little premium.
- Do not spend a lot of money for a little protection.
- Do not consider insurance a substitute for loss control.

5-3. When insurance takes the place of loss control, the insured passes the cost of absorbing additional losses to the insurer and is trading dollars with the insurer. It may be more economical to spend dollars on a loss control program that will prevent and reduce losses and lower the long-term cost of insurance and the risk management program.

5-4. a. Chris has ignored the informal guideline that insurance should not be used as a substitute for loss control.

b. Chris should have attempted to identify the reasons for the increased frequency in physical damage losses. If the reasons for the increased loss frequency had been identified, Chris could have implemented loss control techniques—such as a driver safety program—that might have remedied the real problem instead of merely trading dollars with the insurer.

Educational Objective 6

6-1. To implement chosen risk management techniques, a risk manager must make the following decisions:
- What should be done
- Who should be responsible
- How to communicate the risk management information
- How to allocate the costs of the risk management program

6-2. Risk managers usually do not have complete authority to implement risk management techniques and must depend on others for implementation based on the risk manager's advice.

6-3. Risk management departments of large organizations generally rely on a risk management manual to inform others of how to identify new loss exposures, what risk management techniques are currently in place, how to report insurance claims, and other important information.

Educational Objective 7

7-1. The risk manager monitors a risk management program by periodically identifying and analyzing new and existing loss exposures and then reexamining, selecting, and implementing appropriate risk management techniques.

7-2. Monitoring a risk management program entails handling routine matters, such as updating fleets of vehicles, to making complex decisions about new activities to initiate or avoid.

7-3. A household or an organization should thoroughly review its insurance program with its agent or broker each year because decisions regarding insurance are usually interrelated with other risk management techniques. As a result, any change in this area of the risk management program affects the other areas.

7-4. James will return to the original step in the risk management process to identify new loss exposures that must be addressed. He should also determine whether the loss control measures implemented have reduced the number of accidents or injuries. If they have not, he should consider implementing corrective actions.

Educational Objective 8

8-1. A business can benefit from risk management in the following ways:
- Improved access to affordable insurance
- Increased opportunities
- Achievement of business goals

8-2. Individuals and families can benefit from risk management in the following ways:
- Ability to cope more effectively with financial disasters
- Greater peace of mind
- Reduction in expenses
- Incentive to take more chances and make more aggressive decisions
- Ability to continue activities following an accident or other loss

8-3. Society as a whole benefits from risk management in the following ways:
- Stimulation of economic growth
- Reduction in the number of persons dependent on society for support
- Fewer disruptions in the economic and social environment

8-4. Insurers benefit from risk management in the following ways:
- Risk management creates a positive effect on an insurer's underwriting results, loss ratio, and overall profitability.
- Risk management provides more thoughtful consumers of insurance.
- Risk management creates innovative products and competitive prices and services.
- Risk management helps insurers obtain the respect and business of risk managers and companies that have a risk management program.

8-5.
- Coping with financial disasters—"If you cause an accident, the insurance will pay for the damage to the other vehicles and for the injuries to the other passengers. Otherwise, they may sue you personally."
- Enjoying greater peace of mind—"With insurance, you will not have to worry about being held financially responsible for damages to others."
- Continuing activities following an accident—"If you purchase insurance to cover your car, you will be able to repair this vehicle or buy another one if this one is damaged in an accident."

Educational Objective 9

9-1. a. The Garcias identified their property and liability loss exposures as follows:
- Listed loss exposures
- Did a physical inspection of their home to identify additional loss exposures
- Inventoried their household contents
- Listed their potential liability exposures

b. The Garcias analyzed their loss exposures as follows:
- Analyzed all the loss exposures identified and attempted to determine which ones could cause the most frequent or most severe losses

c. They examined the following risk management techniques:
- Avoidance—Eliminate the chance of loss by disposing of an existing loss exposure or by not assuming new exposure
- Loss control—Lower frequency (number) and/or severity (cost) of losses
- Retention—Retain all or part of a loss exposure (intentionally or unintentionally)
- Insurance—Transfer financial consequences of specified losses from one party to an insurer in exchange for a specified fee
- Noninsurance transfer—Transfer potential financial consequences of a loss exposure from one party to another party that is not an insurer

d. They selected the following risk management techniques appropriate for the family:
- Avoidance—Should they buy a house near the river?
- Loss control—Should they add smoke detectors, locks, or a burglar alarm system?
- Retention—Should they retain part of their loss exposures?
- Insurance—Should they purchase additional insurance?

e. They implemented the following selected risk management techniques:
- Avoidance—Decided not to purchase the house near the river
- Loss control—Installed locks and smoke detectors
- Retention—Increased deductibles to retain part of the saxophone loss exposure
- Insurance—Purchased umbrella insurance for large liability losses

f. They monitored and revised their risk management program as follows:
- They plan to do another physical inspection and inventory at the time of homeowners policy renewal or major life changes
- They modified their risk management program to include human loss exposures

9-2. The Garcia family decided not to specifically insure their daughter's saxophone because their homeowners policy already covered it for fire, theft, lightning, and other causes of loss.

9-3. The Garcia family would apply the retention technique if their daughter lost or damaged her saxophone by replacing it with money from their personal funds, making their daughter earn money to replace it, or deciding not to buy a new one.

Exam Information

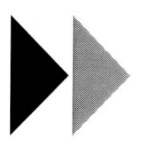

About Institutes Exams

Exam questions are based on the Educational Objectives stated in the course guide and textbook. The exam is designed to measure whether you have met those Educational Objectives. The exam does not test every Educational Objective. Instead, it tests over a balanced sample of Educational Objectives.

How to Prepare for Institutes Exams

What can you do to prepare for an Institutes exam? Students who pass Institute exams do the following:

- Use the assigned study materials. Focus your study on the Educational Objectives presented at the beginning of each course guide assignment. Thoroughly read the textbook and any other assigned materials, and then complete the course guide exercises. Choose a study method that best suits your needs; for example, participate in a traditional class, online class, or informal study group; or study on your own. Use the Institutes' SMART Study Aids (if available) for practice and review. If this course has an associated SMART Online Practice Exams product, you will find an access code on the inside back cover of this course guide. This access code allows you to print (in PDF format) a full practice exam and to take additional online practice exams that will simulate an actual credentialing exam.

- Become familiar with the types of test questions asked on the exam. The practice exam in this course guide or in the SMART Online Practice Exams product will help you understand the different types of questions you will encounter on the exam.

- Maximize your test-taking time. Successful students use the sample exam in the course guide or in the SMART Online Practice Exams product to practice pacing themselves. Learning how to manage your time during the exam ensures that you will complete all of the test questions in the time allotted.

Types of Exam Questions

The exam for this course consists of objective questions of several types.

The Correct-Answer Type

In this type of question, the question stem is followed by four responses, one of which is absolutely correct. Select the *correct* answer.

> Which one of the following persons evaluates requests for insurance to determine which applicants are accepted and which are rejected?
>
> a. The premium auditor
>
> b. The loss control representative
>
> c. The underwriter
>
> d. The risk manager

The Best-Answer Type

In this type of question, the question stem is followed by four responses, only one of which is best, given the statement made or facts provided in the stem. Select the *best* answer.

> Several people within an insurer might be involved in determining whether an applicant for insurance is accepted. Which one of the following positions is primarily responsible for determining whether an applicant for insurance is accepted?
>
> a. The loss control representative
>
> b. The customer service representative
>
> c. The underwriter
>
> d. The premium auditor

The Incomplete-Statement or Sentence-Completion Type

In this type of question, the last part of the question stem consists of a portion of a statement rather than a direct question. Select the phrase that *correctly* or *best* completes the sentence.

> Residual market plans designed for individuals who are unable to obtain insurance on their personal property in the voluntary market are called
>
> a. VIN plans.
> b. Self-insured retention plans.
> c. Premium discount plans.
> d. FAIR plans.

"All of the Above" Type

In this type of question, only one of the first three answers could be correct, or all three might be correct, in which case the best answer would be "All of the above." Read all the answers and select the *best* answer.

> When a large commercial insured's policy is up for renewal, who is likely to provide input to the renewal decision process?
>
> a. The underwriter
> b. The loss control representative
> c. The producer
> d. All of the above

"All of the following, EXCEPT:" Type

In this type of question, responses include three correct answers and one answer that is incorrect or is clearly the least correct. Select the *incorrect* or *least correct* answer.

> All of the following adjust insurance claims, EXCEPT:
>
> a. Insurer claim representatives
> b. Premium auditors
> c. Producers
> d. Independent adjusters